2016

G

MW00681394

We would be honored to have your Best Day.

My
BEST
DAY
Thank you.

PRO FOOTBALL

H-949-645-8109

A collection of responses from former and current players and coaches

MARK KEYS

Always
Mark Keys

M K
C E
C Y
O S
O
L
PRESS

McCool Keys Press
5308 Neptune
Newport Beach, CA 92663

Individual Sales, This book is available through most bookstores or can be ordered directly from McCool Keys Press at the address above.

Quantity Sales. Special discounts are available on quantity purchases by corporations, associations, and others. For details, contact the "Special Sales Department" at the publisher's address above.

Printed in the United States of America.

Library of Congress Cataloging-in-Publication Data is available from the publisher.

ISBN 978-0-9897878-1-9

Cover Design Concept by Mark Keys & Kendall Roderick
Cover Photos: Thank you ESPN for sharing your library

Cover design and text design by Kendall Roderick (RMind-Design.com)

The text for this book is set in Century

Dedicated to Jim Helfrich and Paul Salata; two men I have always looked up and admired.

A special Thank You to Mary Ann Easterling, who wrote to me on behalf of her husband, Ray Easterling. He, along with so many other pro players, struggled with the pain and after effects of the game.

Sam Farmer, LA Times Sports Writer—your articles have kept me inspired, and the feature on me lead to the ESPN special...I will forever be grateful.

And for inspiration, thank you Frank Sinatra & Dean Martin for your music & films, Kirk Douglas, Burt Lancaster & Jerry Lewis for your movies, Bob Newhart for your TV shows and films, and Steve & Ed Sabol at NFL Films.

In loving memory of my Aunt, Lorene Kerr, and my friend Tommy Mason, who was there for me with every phone call. In memory of David "Deacon" Jones who I got to know over the years; who was someone I would pretend to be when I played football on the beach with my friends as a kid. In memory of Ed Modzelewski, Bob St. Clair, and Chuck Bednarik, as well as all the players who have passed and took the time to write me back; they were all special and inspirational.

FORWARD:

I am always humbled when I meet someone and they tell me they've followed my career and admire me.

I met Mark & his lovely wife, Laurie, at the Frank Sinatra Golf Classic and was truly honored when he asked me to write the forward for his latest book.

God gave me a healthy mind and body and athletic talent which I worked hard for Him to be my best in my NFL career.

My Best Day is every day I can do something, no matter how small, for someone else. Writing and public speaking are not my better gifts, but the love of God and serving others will always be a top priority in my life.

For many years I have played in celebrity/charity golf events like the one where I met Mark and his family. It's not about golf, it's about giving back. At the Frank Sinatra Classic we have an opportunity to visit the children's hospital. What a joy it is to know that these beautiful children are being loved and nurtured as they are being treated and cared for each day.

—JIM TAYLOR
Green Bay Packer & New Orleans Saint, NFL Hall of Fame Running Back

Every day, buddy, everyday

**— TIAINA BAUL
"JUNIOR" SEAU JR.**
*San Diego Chargers, Hall of
Fame Linebacker, 12-time
Pro Bowl Selection*

As I said, my best day is when I am able to give to others. At hundreds of golf outings, I feel good when I can contribute in some small way to help raise much needed funds for cancer centers, heart patients, children's hospitals, cystic fibrosis, youth programs, etc.

I had a stoke five years ago, and through the grace of God, and the help of some wonderful doctors and support of my beautiful wife, Helen, and my family, I survived. It made me want to get out of that hospital as fast as I could. I knew God had more work for me.

One football best day was being put into the Pro football Hall of Fame and being picked as MVP of 1962 player of the year.

Thank you for the privilege of being a part of your inspiring book.

— **JIM TAYLOR**
Green Bay Packer & New Orleans Saint, NFL Hall of Fame Running Back

I finished reading the letter you had sent and must admit that it had provoked a great deal of thought. Some people would say it was the day the Bears won the Super Bowl in 1985, and still others might argue that it was the day I entered the NFL.

After reflecting upon my career, I feel my best day was the day my son inducted me into the Pro football Hall of Fame on July 31, 1993 in Canton Ohio. It meant a great deal to have my son by my side and be a part of that very special occasion. I felt emotions that no record or championship could ever bring.

—WALTER PAYTON

*Chicago Bears, Nine-Time
Pro Bowler, Hall of Fame
Running Back*

My Best Day was being elected to the Pro Football Hall of Fame in 1990.

—BOB ST. CLAIR
San Francisco 49ers, Five-Time Pro Bowler, NFL 1950s All-Decade Team, Hall of Fame Offensive Tackle

The day Alecia & I were married

—TOM LANDRY
*New York Giants, Punter, Corner
Back, Quarterback, Running
Back, Dallas Cowboys, Hall of
Fame Football Coach*

My best day athletically would be my high school game where I scored five touchdowns. My grandpa was dying of cancer at the time so I dedicated that game to him and my dad walked me out. Another best day was being inducted into the football Hall of Fame.

—MARCUS ALLEN
Los Angeles Raider, KC Chiefs, 6 Time Pro Bowler, Hall of Fame Running Back

My best day is always our great win as a Packer and our 37-0 win over the Giants-Coach Lombardi was the toughest and Greatest Coach of all time. Keep up the great outlook, you are a great man and a fun-loving Sports Fan. GO PACKERS!

P.S.: My greatest honor was playing on 6 world championships. I am also glad that Brett Farve is playing again (2008)

—FUZZY THURSTON
Green Bay Packer Hall of Fame
Guard Super Bowl Champions I,
II & XXXI

My Best Day was playing with the Rams, and after retiring, I was able to announce with Dick Enberg, and it gave the opportunity to act in TV & films...all good days.

—MERLIN OLSEN
Los Angeles Rams, Four-teen-Time Pro Bowler, Hall of Fame Defensive Tackle

(My dad's) best day was when he was playing the Eagles against the Giants in New York, and the Giants were down 24-0 at the half. The Giants winning, 26-24. They gave the game ball to my dad, and all the players and coaches signed it, I still have the ball.

I was born during the game, and delivered by the team doctor.

Another best day was his greatest game as a Giant in the 17-9 win at Cleveland.

—BILL "Walleye" ALBRIGHT
New York Giants, CFL All Star
1955 & 1956, Guard (As told by
his daughter Kristine Albright
Hengel & Son-In-Law
Nick Hengel)

All days are my best days...to be able to shoot bas-
kets and putt on a golf course with friends like today, here at The Deacon Jones Fundraiser, former
teammates and to watch football? Its the best.

—OLLIE MATSON
*Chicago Cardinals, Philadelphia
Eagles Halfback, Six-time Pro
Bowler, 1956 Pro Bowl MVP*

The best days of my life were the birth of all of my children and the day I was married. The best day of my life was also the day I was baptized in 1990 in Maine. My best day career-wise was the day we defeated the Green Bay Packers to win Super Bowl XXXII. Certainly, I cannot compare that day or the impact on my life with the first events, but it was special. To work that long and hard and finally be victorious was fulfilling.

—RICK DENNISON
Denver Broncos, Linebacker,
Baltimore Ravens, Denver
Broncos Assistant Coach

It is indeed wonderful to reflect on what we have rather than what we don't have! My best day was the day I accepted Jesus Christ as my personal Savior. That is the day I was assured of my salvation.

—VINCE TOBIN

Arizona Cardinals Head Coach, Green Bay Packers, Chicago Bears Assistant Coach

Every day is my best day!

—HARRY CARSON
NY Giants, 9 Time Pro Bowl,
Hall of Fame Linebacker

My Best Day as a player was the "Ice Bowl" game in which I scored the 1st two Packers touchdown's- this will win you many trivia contests because most people do not remember anything about that game except the sneak to win the game at the end.

—BOYD DOWLER

Green Bay Packers, Washington Redskins, Two-Time Pro Bowl Wide Receiver

My Best Day ever, as a professional football player, was against the Super Bowl Champions New York Giants, in the 1987 opening game at Soldier Field against our Chicago Bears. The team performed extremely well, and I had a very solid game, throwing 3 touchdown passes helping our team win a dominating performance. What made it extra special was the head coach for the Giants was Bill Parcells, a former teammate of my fathers' at Wichita State University Football Team.

—**MIKE TOMCZAK**

Chicago Bears, Pittsburg Steelers, Quarterback, Super Bowl XX Champion

I have had a number of best days:

1. The day I received my first NFL head coaching job with the Carolina Panthers
2. The day I married my lovely wife Karen
3. The day we beat the Pittsburg Steelers to clinch the first NFL West Championship
4. The day we beat the Dallas Cowboys in the 1996 playoffs

—DOM CAPERS

Carolina Panther& Houston Texans Head Coach, Green Bay Packers Assistant Defensive Coach, Super Bowl Champ XLV

I loved that I worked for the Cleveland Browns for 40 years. My best game was in the 1964 championship game when we beat the Baltimore Colts 27-10. The month of June at the grounds practice field were the best of times. Also coaching at the University of Santa Clara and coaching at Purdue University with Weeb Eubanks. I was one of four boys and the oldest, we lived and died playing football. I loved playing for the Browns.

—ED ULSINKI

Cleveland Browns, Guard,
Cleveland Browns Assistant
Coach As told by his daughter,
Karen Ulsinki

My best day was when the Saints won their very first game in Saints history. The game was versus Eagles in 1967. I was associated press player of the week and I scored three touchdowns. I ran 91 yards on the opening kickoff, I returned a fumble for a 30 yard score as well as a 50 yard final game winning pass reception. I loved the Cleveland Browns and the championship in 1964. But my best day was with the New Orleans Saints, thanks for asking.

—**WALT "Flea" ROBERTS**
Cleveland Browns, Washington Redskins, Wide Receiver

I would say that my best day in 1969 when the Washington Redskins played the Chicago Bears at Wrigley Field. It was the only professional game my family went to see me in person and it was a special day. My roommate, Sonny Jurgenson, knew the family was there and basically said "well, you get open and I'll get it to you" well he was true to his word as he threw a good number of passes my way, including three touchdown passes and it was my best day in the NFL and as an NFL player.

—PAT RICHTER
Denver Broncos, Washington Redskins, Punter/Wide Receiver, 1st round draft choice 1963

My best day was Christmas Eve 2012 when I left the office and the light is off in Chucks office. (I finally left after Chuck) Best Christmas ever! My second best day was when Andrew and Reggie hooked up for a game-winning touchdown versus Green Bay to win the game and they gave Chuck the game ball.

—BRUCE ARIANS

Indianapolis Colts Assistant Coach, 2012 Coach of the Year Arizona Cardinals, Head Coach. 2x Coach of the Year- 2012 & 2014

My greatest day in theNFL, huh? Well there were two of them I will let you decide. For the first one was when the general manager of the 49ers, Dwight Clark, (from the catch)... Told me I was going to start next year because they were going to cut one of the two Pro Bowls safeties I had been backing up for three years. I almost cried. My own career fortunately ended just a month later due to severe knee injury on special teams. But I will never forget that conversation with my childhood hero Dwight Clark of what was almost was. All the hard work was then worth it... My backup ended up going to several Pro Bowls the next year and signed a 15+ million dollar contract but all he needed was what Dwight Clark. Surreal feeling...

My next greatest day probably created the last one I just mentioned. So the back story was it was late August 1997 and our Super Bowl winning coach had just been fired for a new younger energetic guy. The new guy like most coaches wanted to make his mark immediately, since almost every person on the team was a Pro Bowler or former Pro Bowler the starters were safe with the media and the players were all talking about how the new coaches can clean house or cut all the backups, which he did. Just when I thought things couldn't get any worse they did. Our coach appeared to have been avoiding me through which really discouraged me; then one day he got stuck with me in an elevator. I said hi. Immediately said you're one of those USC guys. I probably said yes I was. He said yeah well they fired me on Christmas Eve. He then abruptly left the elevator.

I believe it was during a bowl game in Orlando in the late 80s when that staff got fired after a bowl game. I knew then that my days were limited since he had ax to grind against my alma mater. Then when I was the last in camp I got to the locker room. It was usually the first one they are the last one to leave. He walked up to me and said he was sorry for what it said in the paper today. I told him I had read the paper. He said he told reporters that I probably wasn't going make the team. He then said the management made him come say sorry to me for saying that. They had a strict policy against making comments like that I guess. I remember he never looked me in the eye when he said sorry.

Then our final scrimmage before Final Cut together as a team and said there were a few players that this scrimmage was that a make or break them. I knew who he was talking to... So was the number one offense in the NFL with Steve, Jerry

Rice, Brent Jones and a young Terrell Owens etc...
against me and the rest of the number two 49ers
defense. I knew something was up when the head
coach normally only helped with the offense called
our defense for us and it was an odd one. One we
rarely played. It matched me at safety and a man-
to-man coverage against the greatest wide receiver of all time, Jerry Rice. On the play Jerry ran a
tricky post route. I knew it was going to be him
for a lot of reasons but thanks to my days as a cornerback at USC for the great coach Bobby April
I was prepared. On the USC baseball team also
reworked and speed turns in the outfield all the
time which really helped as well. So when Steve
Young pump faked for the post and I bit, I gave
a hard speed turn to the corner and made a diving catch over Jerry's shoulder and intercepted
the pass. The entire defense went crazy as well
as thousands of them along the sidelines. I looked
over at the new head coach and he looked shocked.

You see Steve and Jerry were in their prime I
wasn't sure that Steve Young threw an interception during the entire training camp. Thousands
of passes and no interceptions. It was one of those
moments in my life I will never forget. Then after
the number one 49er defense met the number two
49er offense players I was back out there again

against Jerry and Steve and the rest of the highest scoring offense in the NFL. I was still on high alert as I knew my testing was not complete. After a few running plays and a penalty it was third and long. I saw this head coach walked into the huddle and whisper something to the quarterback coach who's calling the place where the coach yelled out for us to go to another uncharacteristic defense. Once again I was matched up on Jerry Rice in a man-to-man coverage. As he quickly approached, I thought to myself, well he knows who is getting the ball so just stay with him. This time he broke his route to the corner hard and I bit again. He then broke to the post in the middle of the field. This time I went into my speed turn, I slipped, my finger got caught in the turf and I broke it. But when your career is on the line there isn't much time for whining so I stayed after Jerry's downfield shoulder. After gaining some ground on the legend, I looked up into the sky and it was a perfectly thrown ball, with a tight spiral, heading right for Jerry's outstretched hands. So I timed my leap luckily just right, jumped as high as I could with one hand outstretched and made a one-handed interception over Jerry Rice. I hit the ground hard but it didn't matter. It didn't matter that my finger was pointing a different direction that I was in a lot of pain. I just made the two greatest plays my entire life against two of the greatest players in sports history and save my job. Apparently Jerry and Steve were two of the many guys that went into the new coaches offices and said, " You can't cut Salmon, we need him." I thought it was such a classy move of those two players and a few others that stood up for me that day. I still get goose bumps telling that story the greatest day of my career — Fight On!

—MIKE SALMON
San Francisco 49ers,
Defensive Back

My best day of my career was being drafted by the Chicago Bears. I always knew I could achieve the top rung in football by quarterbacking a professional football team. All the hard knocks, occasional exposure to racisms as well as nay-sayers I held my own in the league. The icing on the cake is that I still hold the record for the only Chicago Bear to achieve a "perfect quarterback rating" for our game against Green Bay in 1980. I completed 18 of 22 passes, with three touchdowns and passed for 316 yards. What a great day!

—VINCE EVANS
*Chicago Bears, LA/Oakland
Raiders Quarterback*

I guess my best day was a series of three games back to back in 1968. We played in Philly and the old stadium during the "Joe must go" era. It had rained a lot and they had put straw on the field and it was a quagmire. Sloppiest I ever tried to kick in. I don't think I made a single kick during warm-up but during the game I went five for five. They weren't very long but we won the game. The next week we played Minnesota at WrigleyField. It was cold that day and with three seconds left in the game I made a 48 yarder to win the game that was my first field goal to actually win a game. What a great feeling! Then the next week we go to Green Bay. The score is tied ten times and with 20 seconds left to play Green Bay kicked from deep INTO their end zone and we got a fair catch on the 43 yard line. Our coach called for a free kick which none of us ever heard of. We lined up like a kickoff which Richie Petitbon held and with no one rushing I made a 43 yarder that won the game. That is still in the record books. I had my best year that year (nothing compared to today's kickers) those three games were my best days.

—MAC PERCIVAL
Chicago Bears, Dallas
Cowboys, Kicker

Every day I wake up!

—EJ HOLUB
*Dallas Cowboys, KC Chiefs,
Linebacker, 5-Time AFL All
Star Center*

I got to say my best day was in 2007. Coming from Oakland there was a bad taste in my mouth. Being able to team with Tom Brady and Josh McDaniels...we made great things happen. And Bill Belichick was coming off spy gate it; was like "forget everybody, focus on us,let's try to make it happen." The Giants spoil our undefeated season of course. To this day I haven't even watched some of that game. Since I was six years old, I don't think I couldn't have wanted to win a championship more than that year at San Francisco. Man, I get tired of the 72 Dolphins and that trash talk.

—RANDY MOSS

San Francisco 49ers, Oakland
Raiders, New England Patriots,
Minnesota Vikings7-Time Pro
Bowler & MVP Pro Bowl 1999
Wide Receiver

When you ask for my best day, many days could fill in that blank. Just walking on the field playing in the NFL in the 1970s was a privilege. I guess the best day was winning Super Bowl V. Not that it was my best performance but in being a European standing in the bowl, alongside was Johnny Unitas, John McKay etc. that made it special.

—NORMAN BULAICH
Baltimore Colts, Miami Dolphins, Pro Bowl Running Back

One of my best days in football was opening day September 9, 2011. It was the ten-year anniversary of September 11. We Played the Bills on Sunday night and to a national TV audience. It was agreed, and again we came down the field and in the fourth quarter with only 50 seconds, remaining trailing 24-17 Joe McKnight blocked a Dallas punt and was picked up by Isaiah Thompson and ran in for the game-tying touchdown. Then with only three seconds left in the game; the next play I kicked a 50 yard field goal to win the game. It was a great game, great special team's game and a great New York night.

—MIKE WESTHOFF
New York Jets, Miami Dolphins,
Baltimore Colts Assistant Coach

Thank you for considering me for your best day books. One of my best day memories has to do with catching a touchdown pass against the Chicago Bears. I took my father-in-law to one of our home games and got him a field pass to go in the field and take pictures. Shortly after that season he passed away. A couple of months later as I received a copy of that picture. To my shock and surprise the picture of me catching the pass had been my father-in-law taking a picture of me from the end zone. My best day was that day.

— JIM GIBBONS
Detroit Lions, Three-Time Pro BowlTight End

In high school we went to the state championships in football and basketball, but lost both times. In college Oklahoma University

We went to the big eight but lost to Alabama in the Orange bowl. In professional football I've spent 13 years with Dallas, we lost Bowl VI but I was injured and didn't play. We went to Super Bowl X to be defeated by the Pittsburgh Steelers. Then Dallas went to Super Bowl XII and beat the Denver Broncos which happened to be my last day. I had announced my retirement prior to the last regular-season game at home in Dallas why is this is my best day? "The last game I played was the first game I played in that we won all the marbles!"

—RALPH NEELY
Dallas Cowboys, Four-Time
All Pro, All- Decade Team
1960's,Tackle

My best day is threefold: The day I signed a contract with LA Rams in 1959 Pete Rozelle. To my first ever touchdown passes as a pro in 1964 the Raiders we were playing the New York Titans at the old Polo grounds. I played for Tom Flores. I signed a pro baseball contract with the Cincinnati Reds in Newport Beach in 1955. Yes I was very happy kid then and will never forget any of them.

—AL HOISINGTON
Oakland Raiders, Buffalo Bills,
LA Rams Quarterback

Winning the Heisman trophy was certainly a unique experience and vastly different from some of the other good days: getting married, children being born, parent's 40th wedding anniversary.

—JOHN CAPPELLETTI

LA Rams, San Diego Charger
1st Round Draft Pick 1974,
Running Back

I love football. On the floor of the cavernous Memorial Coliseum in Los Angeles Miami quarterback Bob Griese ducked his head into the Dolphin huddle. Before Bob uttered a single syllable I knew what play he was going to call, I had been waiting to hear it from the moment I picked up a football for the first time a couple decades before. I had dreamed of this moment.

The date was January 14, 1973 in Southern California. But this wasn't just any Sunday afternoon. It was Super Bowl Sunday! The seventh Super Bowl in NFL history to match the undefeated Miami Dolphins coached by Don Shula and coach George Allen's over the Hill gang Washington Redskins. It was the most important game of my football life culmination of years of hard work and dedication.

But up to this point in time the NFL's showcase event had been quite ordinary. As the first quarter ticked away, the game was scoreless. With time running out in the opening period, the Dolphins had stage our first real threat of the afternoon, having driven the ball from our own 37 yard line to the Redskins 28 yard line. To continue the drive, we needed another first down. Facing a third-and-six situation, we knew the Redskins defense was likely to set it we called a split coverage pass defense. In that alignment, cornerback Mike Bass and free safety Roosevelt Taylor would double team cover Paul Warfield, our multiple time All-Pro and future Hall of Famer and strong safety, Brig Owens would pick up the tight end, Marv Fleming, in single coverage. That left Pat Fischer, the Redskins 5'9" 170 pound cornerback, on me, one-on-one. I had studied Fischer in films, and knew if I took three quick steps before making my break I could pull Fischer. I went to Bob Griese explaining my reasoning and showed him how I wanted to execute the post corner against the Redskins defense. He agreed and we practiced it in the two weeks before the Super Bowl in the huddle and I knew Bob was going to call the play and it was time for me to execute. Brown right 60 double Q on two he said in the huddle. Ready break! I ran to the right of the formation. As I knew he would, Fischer lined up opposite me. As Bob barked out the signals I remain focused on the task at hand. Finally I heard Bob say hut-hut! And I broke down the field. In the few seconds of followed everything went just as we practiced. In my head I counted my five strides toward the goalposts and Fischer committed to what he thought was going to be a straight post pattern. With his momentum now going towards his right I pivoted back toward the corner of the end zone. I instinctively knew Fischer had been fooled. As I wheeled back around towards the corner, I brought my head around as well, towards Bob in the pocket. There it was! The football..floating over the outstretched hands of Redskins linebacker Harold McClinton. It was a beautiful thing to behold! The ball thudded against my chest around the 6 yard line, and I turned toward the goal. I hadn't even taken two steps before Fischer grabbed me around my upper body. We wrestled the final few yards before I push the ball just inside the flag at the corner of the end zone. I had scored the first touchdown of Super Bowl VII. What a moment! Our kicker, Garo Yepremian, added the extra point. We defeated the Washington Redskins that day, 14 to 7, to complete the first and (only undefeated) season 17 to 0 in NFL history.

—HOWARD TWILLEY
Miami Dolphins, College Hall of Fame, Wide Receiver

One of my best days was a phone call from Baltimore Colts general manager, Steve Rosenbloom, asking me how did I feel about being the Colts #1 draft pick? Meeting and playing with the late, legendary great Quarterback, Johnny Unitas and playing in Super Bowl V against the Dallas Cowboys. But, my best day in the NFL was catching Johnny Unitas's last touchdown pass for 63 yards in Memorial Stadium in Baltimore against the Buffalo Bills in 1972.

—EDDIE HINTON
Houston Oilers, Baltimore Colts,
1st Round Pick 1969, Receiver

I have had many best days. I played college at the University of Houston. I joined the Detroit Lions as an undrafted free agent in 1961 where I spent seven years with Detroit. 1962 I was NFL's leading punt returner with 29 punts for 457 yards. In 1965 I return punts and kickoffs and played wide receiver. I led the NFL in receiving yards with 1266 on 67 catches in 1966. I was the third wide receiver in NFL history to score a touchdown on a 99 yard pass play and I caught it from Karl Sweetan in our game against Baltimore Colts on October 16. I played in two NFL Pro Bowls and made the AP – UPI All-Pro 1966. My final season was with the New England Patriots. I had a career average of 25.7 on kickoff returns and 100 yarder for a touchdown in Chicago in 1961. I was also inducted into Louisiana's Sports Hall of Fame. All of these attributes and accolades in my life filled with many best days.

—PAT STUDSTILL
Detroit Lions, L.A. Rams,
2-Time Pro Bowler, Wide
Receiver& Punter

When I accepted Jesus as my Lord and Savior in spring of 1975.When I married my wife. Also when we had our four children (tied times four)

—BOB BREUNIG

Dallas Cowboys, Three-Time
Pro Bowl Linebacker

I had many great days throughout my career but the greatest days were the ones that I shared with God, Family, and Friends.

—MYRON POTTIOS
LA Rams, Pittsburg Steelers,
Three-Time Pro Bowl
Linebacker

My best day occurred on Sunday, January 17, 1971 the Baltimore Colts became world champions by defeating the Dallas Cowboys in the Super Bowl. It was great to win the game and it erased any doubts that might have been prevalent after the loss in Super Bowl Three to the New York Jets. The game was the greatest joy, and surrounding the event was terrific but the true game of life best day was revealed that afternoon to me by my wife Lorraine. In 1966 our second child Julie was born with down syndrome, a form of mental retardation. After several years of debating about having another child we decided to move ahead. The medical team has suggested that my wife submit to several new tests trying to try and rule out the birth of another Downs baby. The tests were performed in early December 1971 wife received results just prior to the game but decided to hold back and telling me so I could be fully focused on the task at. So after the game she advised me that all the tests were negative and that we were going to have another healthy baby girl that was named Kristen.

Today my older daughter is the mother of three, senior VPs at Fidelity Investments. Julie is 43 and still living at home with us and attends the sheltered workshop which includes living life to the fullest. Kristen, I'm happy to say, devoted her life to teaching special needs teacher truly dedicated to her career. How's that for a best day.

—**DAN SULLIVAN**
Baltimore Colts, 1961 Scanlan Winner, Tackle, Guard

My best day was in Cleveland. As we came out onto the field, I was greatly surprised when I saw my high school coach coming across the field. It was Tommy Hewitt who was a national football referee. I was awestruck and when Tommy Hewitt saw me asked me, "what the hell are you doing here?" and we shook hands.

—GEORGE SPETH
Detroit Lions, Lineman & Tackle

In 1970 there was only one game on television, every Sunday at 2 PM. ABC had scheduled the Rams against the Jets expecting the fearsome foursome of Deacon Jones, Merlin Olsen, Lamar Lundy, and Rosie Grier to be pitted against Joe Namath. The only problem was that Namath got hurt several weeks earlier and Al Woodall (who?) was playing for the Jets, who were now a 17 point underdog. I threw three touchdown passes and upset the Rams 32 to 20 in the LA Coliseum on national television.

—AL WOODALL
NY Jets, Round 2 Draft Choice
1969, Quarterback

51

My best personal day in the NFL was against the New York Jets. It was a year after we had lost to them in Super Bowl III. I had three interceptions and one returned for a touchdown.

—JERRY LOGAN
Baltimore Colts, Three-Time
Pro Bowl Safety

My best day in sports was December 27, 1964 when we beat the Baltimore Colts 27-0. We were a 17 point underdog. No one expected us, or me, to have a great day. I ended up with five catches for 130 yards and three touchdowns, plus punting for a 42 yard average. I won the MVP and a 1965 Corvette... wish I still had it.

—GARY COLLINS
Cleveland Browns, Two-Time
Pro Bowler, NFL 1960s All
Decade Team, Wide
Receiver/Punter

My best day when I played for the New York Giants vs. the Dallas Cowboys, Don Meredith was quarterback. I had two interceptions; one for a touchdown. We went on to win, and eventually played for the NFL championship game against the Bears.

—JERRY HILLEBRAND
NY Giants, St Louis Cardinals,
Pittsburg Steelers,Round 2 Draft
Choice 1962, Linebacker

My best day was the game against the Green Bay Packers early in the season at their home field in Green Bay, Wisconsin. I believe it was 1997. I had been trying to play a perfect game for my entire career. A perfect game for me was a total mistake free ball, and no missed calls, drop passes etc.... The game against the Packers was as close if I would ever get. I had over 100 yards rushing, every pass thrown to me, and someone made some great blocks. As a matter of fact I believe I counted for over 80% of our offensive output for that game. It was one of those games where it began and ended with men in the trans-like state that is sort of hard to describe. I believe most people called it being in the zone.

I felt like this a few times in my career but nothing like that Packer game. Everything went great until the very end of the game when I missed a block which actually meant very little to the outcome. I remember being upset after the game for a while but realized it was silly to be mad so I got over it. I walked into the parking lot after the game waiting for a bus and a group of Packers fans called me over to their tailgate area. They offered me a beer and congratulated me on a great game. A classy act by a great group of football fans, it was amazing. From that day on, I actually looked forward to playing our archrivals in the beautiful football stadium of theirs. It was My greatest day and my favorite as a professional football player.

—DARREN NELSON

*Minnesota Vikings, 1st
Round Draft Choice 1982,
Running Back*

My best day in football was returning to the football field 10 month after my, so-called, career ending knee injury in November 1967. After my first exhibition game in 1968, I felt confident that my career would not end.Thus, my best day.

—EMERSON BOOZER
*New York Jets, Baltimore Colts,
1968 World Champion, Two-
Time Pro Bowl Running Back*

Outside of the birth of my children and the day of my marriage, one of my best days of my life in football was the game against St. Louis in 1975 playoff. I had two interceptions and returned one for 65 yards for a touchdown, but the best day of my life in the sports world was when my son Brett, 19, won the US Open of surfing in 2009 at the Huntington Beach pier against the best in the world. There were great waves and thousands of people watching. Even with all that I was able to do in my career, watching my son which gave me a feeling I had never felt before...to see your child do this was the best day of my life.

—BILL SIMPSON
LA Rams, Buffalo Bills, Round 2 Draft Choice 1974, Defensive Back

My best days are hard to single out:

The two world championships in Green Bay.

Going to the LA Rams and being a starter for 10 years.

Meeting and playing with the LA Rams and making lifelong friends.

Retiring and going into coaching with the Philadel-phia Eagles. For 25 years I was with the Eagles – so that gave me 40 years of being in the N.F.L.

—KEN IMAN
Green Bay Packers, L.A. Rams, Center

My best day was in 1972 against the Denver Broncos in Denver. I kicked five field goals with the last one from 43 yards to win the game 36 to 34.

—BRUCE GOSSETT
San Francisco49ers, LA Ram, All NFC 1974, Place Kicker

My best day was when I had the chance to play quarterback in the NFL – Unitas was hurt – our second string quarterback Gary Couzzo was hurt and Coach Shula had no other person to use but me. I had been a quarterback in college but was more of a half back under center – rolling out and either running or throwing the ball. We won the first game versus the Los Angeles Rams and that tied us with Green Bay for our division title. We played on Christmas day in Green Bay and the field goal that tied the game was 'No good". The official blew the call and we went into sudden death game – they kicked a field goal to win. The following year, because of the blown call in our game, goalposts were raised 20 feet higher so the wonderful officials could see better. We then went to the runner-up bowl in Miami and beat the Cowboys 35 to 3 and I won the MVP award. Great team, great challenges and a whole lot of fun

—TOM MATTE
Baltimore Colts, Two-Time Pro Bowl Running Back

I consider my best day was the day that I broke Lou Groza's record for the most field goals in a single year. It was in 1962. The previous record was 23 I made 26. In 1962 I was awarded the Dapper Dan award for the best athlete in Pittsburgh.

—LOU MICHAELS

LA Rams, Green Bay Packers, Defensive Lineman & 2-Time Pro Bowl Place Kicker

There have been a lot of great days in my career, but the one I feel like was my happiest and the most rewarding was the day I came home from the war. When I got home I was afforded an opportunity to finish my senior year of high school, and my senior year of football. At the end of the season I was offered a football scholarship at the University of Alabama. My dream was to play college football, not even thinking about playing in the NFL. My senior year I was drafted by the Pittsburgh Steelers as their first round draft choice. The chances that I received to play at Alabama and for the Steelers made a great training field for becoming a high school football coach.

—TOM CALVIN
Pittsburg Steelers, Halfback

One best day is a hard question. There been so many and most of them have nothing to do with sports. My children being born is one. Long talks I would have with my dad about God before he passed was special. To pick one is hard, too many to count.

—ERIC DICKERSON
Oakland Raiders, Indianapolis Colts, LA Rams, 6-Time Pro Bowler, Hall of Fame Running Back

I am forever humbled. This is the happiest day of my life when I learned I was one of the seven men elected to Hall of Fame in 2013. I have had a lot of very, very good, good days. We've been blessed, the Hall of Fame. But the best day for me really was a summer day when I had been suspended from the NFL and on that day I was in such bad shape strung out on crack cocaine that I can't even remember the date, but I know that if I didn't make that decision that day, I would never have been in the Hall. So it would be easy to say getting into the Hall, but that summer day that I can't even remember because I was in such bad shape and before the Eagles cut me.

—CRIS CARTER
Minnesota Vikings, Philadelphia Eagles, Eight-Time Pro Bowler, Hall of Fame Wide Receiver

The day we played Houston for the American League championship in 1960 was my best day.

—VOLNEY PETERS
*Washington Redskins, Philadelphia Eagles, Pro Bowl
Defensive Tackle*

I have been blessed with the opportunity to play football after growing up in a small town in southern Oklahoma. It is hard for me to pick out my best day, but one was catching a touchdown pass on my first play to win the game with the Philadelphia Eagles in 1947. I was fortunate enough to play with some of the best players ever in NFL and win two world championships.

—NEILL ARMSTRONG
*Minnesota Vikings, Wide
Receiver & Defensive Back*

I believe my best day in the pros was starting the game and playing most of it. In the 40s and 50s "going both ways" was common. Our quarterback was lovingly called the Texas Wonder. One of his best plays was letting our end run to the flag; when all else fails he would throw at me and many times we were successfully.

—TOM BLAKE
New York Bulldogs 1949, Tackle

Although I did not play high school football at Ohio State under Woody Hayes when I attended college, Mel Renfro & John Wooten were the scouts who signed me to my first NFL contract with the Dallas Cowboys in 1979. Coach Tom Landry was the leader of the Dallas Cowboys Football Club. So I guess you could imagine that I have had a lot of best day events. My first game ever was the Hall of Fame in Canton Ohio versus Oakland Raiders and I caught my first punt from Ray Guy. As a rookie defensive back, the first receiver I had to cover was Cliff Branch. The last pre-season game was against Super Bowl championship Pittsburgh Steelers: Terry Bradshaw, Franco Harris, Lynn Swann, Mel Blount, Mean Joe Greene and John Stallworth were just to name a few. I ran a 62 yard punt return that day to set up the winning score and I probably made the Dallas Cowboys on that play alone. The following game was opening day on the road against the St. Louis Cardinals. We won the game 22 to 21 and I ran 47 yards with the kickoff after O.J. Anderson put them ahead with the 68 yard score with 58 seconds left in the game. I made the front of the Dallas Cowboys weekly magazine also. Had a few best days since...I should not been an NFL player.

—WADE MANNING
*Dallas Cowboys, Wide Receiver
& Defensive Back*

My best day came while playing against the LA Rams. I had over 100 yards rushing by halftime. Since it was against the fearsome foursome, it made it special. At the seasons end, the Rams voted me as the best running back they faced that year.

—TOM WOODESHICK

Philadelphia Eagles, St Louis Cardinals, Pro Bowl Running Back

The best day for me, and I've had a lot of them, was in 1974 against the Los Angeles Rams in my hometown of LA. They were my favorite team growing up, even the number 25 that I wore in college was the number used by Bernie Casey when he played for the Rams. The best day was a real nice day playing the Rams, it was my birthday and there were 78 family and friends at the game who had made me birthday signs that night and we beat the Rams 27 to 24. I had three touchdowns and after the game one of my friends knew a lot of the Rams players and they had a party for me.

—STEVE HOLDEN
Cincinnati Bengals, Cleveland Browns, 1st Round Draft Pick, Wide Receiver

I didn't play long- the first game I played and first pass I caught was for a touchdown making it my best day.

—BOB TOPP
*New York Giants, Receiver, First
Team All-Big Ten Conference*

My best day was August 17, 2011 the day my son Kenbrell the second was born. It has definitely been a blessing becoming a father and a little guy that looks to me like no other. I can honestly say the day my son was born, my commitment and dedication to football went to another level. The patience I now have in ways he may never understand ...however that as his father I just knew I had to succeed to ensure a great future for him

—KENBRELL THOMPKINS

New England Patriots, Oakland Raiders, Wide Receiver

The best day for me was being drafted by the Rams in 1959, especially being from a very small college, Arkansas Tech. Next I would say that our game against the Dallas Cowboys in which I was voted NFL defenseman player of the week and I don't even remember the date.

—ED MEADOR
*LA Rams, Six-time Pro Bowl,
Defensive Back*

I thought the last game of 1958 season could be it (a best day) as I was a defensive back and against Pittsburgh and Bobby Layne- I intercepted three passes and was looking forward to 1959. Never played another game on defense!

1959, opening game of the season against the Washington Redskins, I started at right half back on offense. They scored three touchdowns- two rushing and a pass reception. I rushed for a hundred yards and added 40 yards receiving on 10 carries and I kicked seven extra points. That had been my best day.

—BOBBY CONRAD
Dallas Cowboys, Pro Bowl
Wide Receiver

My list consists of ongoing events that made me end this statement with my best day.

1) I was drafted by the 49ers after my stint the US Army, I reported to Moraga California for camp.

2) I was a linebacker and I was obligated to play alongside the great Hardy Brown. Hardy adopted me and from him I learned several tricks on the job.

The most vivid occurred in the Packers game on the task play, Tobin Rote the Green Bay quarterback was back and I noticed that he was looking left. From line-backer I faded to the left and sure enough the ball was headed my direction. Yes..an interception..my first, and to my excitement my idol Hardy Brown, my teacher said "could not of done it any better". The ultimate!!

PS- Always the excitement of chasing Eddie LeBaron, Bobby Layne, etc. leave a life time of memories. Good luck and God bless you and yours.

—TOM STOLHANDSKE
San Francisco 49ers, First Round Draft Pick, Linebacker & Defensive End

During the 1970's, names like Dandy Don, Howard Cosell and Frank Gifford conjured up thoughts of nothing else that "Monday Night Football." As a student at NAIA Division III University of Redlands, we would watch college football all day on Saturday (of course on the television) and the pros on Sunday. Monday night was made special by a cult known as Monday night "highlights".

No ESPN, nor cable channels to air every Pop Warner game in the country existed then so we viewed only the top echelon of athlete on your basic channels. Thanks to my U of R teammates and a much admired coach (Serrao). I was afforded the opportunity to continue my athletic career in the NFL via a fifth round draft choice by the New York Giants. The majority of my playing career took place in Baltimore with the Colts and it was here that I could recall my greatest day.

When you're in your second season as an NFL player, homesickness is still prevalent and, for a brief spell in September of 1979, the city of Redlands was not only on the map, it engulfed my telephone line as well. Sunday afternoon I had caught a short hook pattern against the Tampa Bay Buccaneers and, thanks to a couple of great blocks down field by Mack Alston, took Greg

Landry's pass and turned it up our own sideline for a 67 yard touchdown.

My first professional touchdown sent the game into overtime and launched a bit of a media blitz. The next day I was two minutes late to our special teams meeting and Booter (George Boustellis) had only a glare for me as he opened the locker door (to a round of ching-ching by my special team's compadres). This, and the 100.00 fine which accompanied it was all well worth the evening ahead.

Now, while you'd think that the Memorial Stadium mania which followed the touchdown would account for the "great" in "greatest". It was Howard Cossell's rendition of the play that started the telephone a ringin'. To this day, I wish I cad a copy of his call as he referred to me as the receiver from little Redlands University of Monday Night Football HIghtlights. It still remains in my mind, as hopefully it does with the fans that called that night to say that they had witnessed it, as my greatest day.

—BRIAN DEROO
Baltimore Colts, Wide Receiver

Three things I remember which happened to me as best days.

I was drafted as a defensive back. Two, during my first training camp I was switched to a wide receiver, five years later switched to tight end. Having made the Pro Bowl at two different positions was very satisfying. Also during this time I received the honor of being named MVP by the Maxwell Club. I guess playing three different positions and being selected as All-Pro two of the three was very gratifying. In addition to that, I enjoyed it because it always very nice to reach a level of performance that my fellow players voted for you as the MVP.

—PETE RETZLAFF

Philadelphia Eagles, Five-Time Pro Bowl, Wide Receiver & Tight End

I think my best day maybe it was when I was drafted by the Detroit Lions in 1954. My wife of two months and I were very excited when we got the telegram. We decided to go for a ride out in the country. Coming back after the call, a lady decided to pass on a curve we were coming around and hit us head on with no seatbelts, yet we came out of it pretty good. We are celebrating our 60th anniversary on the 19th of December. When I arrived at camp I worked very hard. A few weeks into practice I received a telegram from my mother-in-law that my teapot arrived with the bow! In other words, my first son had arrived, and that Thomas is a hoot. The last exhibition game we played the Steelers in Buffalo, New York. On the plane back to Detroit the head coach Buddy Parker called me over and said Dewey we would like to keep you but we had everyone back from our championship year. You may go home or Pittsburgh needs defensive ends. I said I did not want to go home I would rather play football. The next morning a quarterback from San José's State and myself were flown to Pittsburgh. I worked very hard again and beat out a young man who had taken a leave of absence from the Marines. I started for 12 games. After the season was over, I was drafted into the Army

—DEWEY BRUNDAGE
Pittsburg Steelers, Defensive End

In 1953 I reported to training camp with the Baltimore Colts. They had just move from Dallas, Texas to Baltimore. I was so excited to be in the Lion's program. I believe we played six exhibition games in those days. No one received pay for the games. We received nothing for meal money, and if you were hurt there was no guarantee that you would be paid. For these, and several other reason, several years later players joined together to form the NFLPA.

During the exhibition season I played in almost all the games. The last game was against the Washington Redskins. I started the game and caught 10 passes and scored two touchdowns. I was sure I'd make the roster with my play. I can't remember the name of the general manager at the time. Because I was literally broke, I went to him to see if I could get an advance in my salary. He informed me that he put me on waivers. I blurted out "Are you crazy" I was picked up off waivers by the Chicago Cardinals and spent five seasons with them. Made the Pro Bowl one year and later played for the Steelers and Browns. I saw the general manager from the Colts several times during my career. The first thing he would say after hello was, "yes I was crazy". I tell you this story because it was one of the most exciting times because of my success in the Redskin game and then the most disappointing the next day, when I was waived.

—GERN NAGLER

Pittsburg Steelers, Cleveland Browns, Pro Bowl End

When Eisenhower was president, I was a young officer in the US Air Force. Pres. Eisenhower was an avid sports fan and he has a luncheon at the White House with current sports figures such as Joe DiMaggio, Rocky Marciano and others of that era. I took my invitation to the commander of our squadron and asked for time off. I told him I have an opportunity to have lunch with the President. His answer was president of what, Remington Brand? I answered, no Sir, The President of the United States. I was then flown from Hamilton Air Force Base in California to Washington DC. Because of football, that was my best day.

—ED MODZELEWSKI

Cleveland Browns, Pittsburg Steelers, First Round Draft Choice 1953 Half Back

Being drafted to by the Los Angeles Rams from a small college town, and making the team for 11 wonderful years.

—DUANE PUTNAM

Los Angeles Rams, Two-Time
Pro Bowl Guard

My best day was winning Super Bowl XXIX and having my two boys on the sideline. It's great to see you overcome adversity... I've always said a quote that success is not determined by material things but determined by how you handle adversity.

—GARY PLUMMER
San Diego Chargers, San Francisco 49ers, Linebacker

My best day professionally was January 30, 1994, Super Bowl XXVIII in Atlanta, Georgia. This day was so special because it was the culmination of so many hours of hard work & preparation for the ultimate game in all of football. Very few get the opportunity to fill their dream, I did!

The game didn't start off too well for the Cowboys. At halftime the score was Dallas 6 (2 field goals by Murray) and Buffalo 13. However, in the second half we exploded for 24 points against the Buffalo Bills 30 to 13. Our defensive play was outstanding, holding Buffalo to 87 yards rushing and zero points in the second half. Emmitt Smith had 30 carries for 132 yards and was the MVP of the game. Troy Aikman, Daryl Johnston and Michael Irvin were tremendous as they had been all year. I was privileged to be the offense line coach that special day. My thanks to a great coaching staff, talented players, and organization for making this day possible.

—HUDSON HOUCK
Seattle Seahawks, LA Rams, Dallas Cowboys, Assistant Coach

My best day? I would have to say the day I got married was my best day! Another best day was the game on October 25, 1964, the final score Minnesota Vikings 27- San Francisco 49ers 22. It was the day I will always remember. The score was back-and-forth. I had about 8 to 10 tackles that day but I did something that many linebackers will never experience.

I had three interceptions that day and of course, I was real proud of my performance. I was awarded the game ball that day and it was the first of 8-10 game balls over 15 year career. Something very unusual happened that day also. It was the day that Jim Marshall ran the wrong way. Needless to say no one heard about my three interceptions.

—ROY WINSTON
Minnesota Vikings, Line Backer
LSU Hall of Fame

My happiest football day was the day I joined the Rams. I played with them for five years, including the 1951 championship game. It gave me a chance play with players such as Tom Fears, Elroy "Crazy Legs" Hirsch, Bob Waterfield, Norm Van Brocklin, Glenn Davis and so many more. It was always my goal to play professional football which I achieved at 19 years old. I have very happy moments remembering the Rams exciting games and the many friends I made in sports.

—JACK FINLAY
Los Angeles Rams, Guard

The day I was drafted into the NFL in 1999 was my best day as a professional athlete. I remember getting the call from the Bengals back stage after seeing a New Year's Eve gospel concert and how good it felt to know that I was the 3rd pick in the draft and what an honor is was to go that high in the draft. For a while that day defined my life: the good; the bad; and the ugly. The symbolic play of my career is probably against the Ravens when I got under Lewis's helmet for a sack to his chinstrap on three-step drop. The draft was a long time ago, but still my best day.

—AKILI SMITH

*Cincinnati Bengals,Green Bay
Packers, Tampa Bay Bucca-
neers, 1st Round Draft Choice
Quarterback*

I can't answer a question for my best day in football, football is a great sport. I've had so many great days playing and experiencing football that wouldn't be fair to just pick one day. I can however, give you a taste of some of my greatest experiences of football. One of the first memories I had that really hooked me on the sport. In 1969 when I watched a game between Ohio State and Michigan. After seeing that game I told my parents I wanted to play football for Michigan. For four years I have plenty of great days which consisted of four Big Ten championships; and one championship in the Orange Bowl. Most of my teammates and friends will tell you my greatest days were the touchdowns that I scored to win again and for setting the record in the Rose Bowl. The next milestone was the day I signed a contract to play for the Buffalo Bills. As a kid I always dreamed of becoming a player in the NFL. April 1978 signature on the contract became a reality. My NFL experience was very short, if the filter dream additional great days for me in football was coaching him watching my son grow and prove to be a player in his own right. Watching him achieve his goals and winning three Rose Bowl championships is a true joy for me.

—CURT STEPHENSON
Buffalo Bills, Receiver

In terms of my most productive on-field performance, it came in 1984 as a running back spe-
cial-teams performer against the Eagles while
playing for the Detroit Lions. That day I amassed
284 total yards including 75+ rushing 75+ kickoff returns and over 125 pass receiving. It was an
all-purpose record for the year, still stands as an
NFL record combining those categories. Another
huge highlight for me was being picked up by the
Washington Redskins in 1985. Washington DC is
my hometown and I got the opportunity to play in
front of my friends and family for the remaining
two years of my career.

—KEN JENKINS
*Detroit Lions, Philadelphia Ea-
gles, Running Back*

My best day is the day I wake up, because I'm still living. As for my best day in football, I've been blessed with many as a personal individual, l meaning my own grading and satisfaction. But one that came early in my college days, and it gained more national attention than any others. My sophomore year at Duke University, and we met in Atlanta, Georgia to play Georgia Tech in November, 1949. This was the first year Duke had gone to the two platoon system. Coach Wade had placed me with the Defensive Unit at End. I had started in the previous games due to injuries to some older players. I had no idea I would start against Georgia Tech. I found out that morning when they were taping up ankles that the coach was going to start me. I was very relaxed and the older players were very good with me and supportive.

I say, football is a team sport and each player has his heart play. One gets the touchdown, run, the tackle, etc. It is because 10 other guys did their job I got more credit than others.

—BLAINE EARON
Detroit Lions, NFL Champions
1952-1953 Defensive Lineman

I think one of the best days for me was Thanks-giving in 1953,in Detroit, was when I had 4 inter-ceptions with two of them being off Bobby Layne also a Texas Longhorn!! As you probably know I have only one good eye. One was removed when I was 10 years old due to an accident. I was only able to play my senior year in high school for the first time. Since I was 15 years old when the Uni-versity of Texas Coaches talked my parents into letting me stay over for two years it really paid off. I got a scholarship to Texas, that lead to the rest of my success in the NFL.

—BOBBY DYLAN
Detroit Lions &
Green Bay Packers

My best day was simple: 1960 championship as a Philadelphia Eagle.

—TED DEAN
Philadelphia Eagles, Minnesota Vikings, Pro Bowl Running Back

What a great spirit, Mark! Keep on knocking. 14 knee surgeries, 1 replacement, 7 fractured fingers, torn rotator cuffs, blah…blah..blah…
Who cares? It's not where you are, but what you've over come

God Bless

—DAN HAMPTON
Chicago Bears, 1982 NFL
Defensive Player of the Year,
Hall of Fame Defensive Tackle,
Defensive End

My Best Day is every day; very simple. Every day I wake up I'm brand new and it doesn't get any better than that.

—PAUL MAGUIRE

San Diego Charger, Buffalo Bills, Three-Time AFL Champion Linebacker

I have a tie in my response. I was fortunate to have played on a National Championship in 1963 at the University of Texas. (first in history of Texas) and a World Championship is 1968 with New York Jets. We were the first AFL team to beat the NFL and that helped bring the merger of both leagues. I also played in the first Monday Night Football game in 1970.

—PETE LAMMONS
New York Jets, AFL & World
Champions 1968,Tight End

I was benched by my Offensive Line coach after a long holdout. His name was Bad Rad. The guy that took my job tore up his knee and I played the last part of the season and went to the Pro Bowl. I never lost my job again. The best part of the story was next year the team wasn't doing well and Bad Rad stated that only two people on the team are playing good enough to win. One was Rich Saul and he said the other one, that I hate to say, is Dennis Harrah. My best moment in sports. At that moment, Rad could kiss my ass.

—DENNIS HARRAH
Los Angeles Rams, Six-Time Pro Bowl Offensive Lineman

My Best Day is each day or the present day at my age you can understand.

—LOU SABAN
Cleveland Browns Two-Time Pro Bowl Linebacker, Denver Broncos, Two-Time AFLCoach of the Year

I was blessed to have many wonderful days and much more than my share of personal and collective success on the gridiron over my almost twenty years of organized football. These memorable gridiron years began in high school at Bakersfield High, proceeded through my years at Stanford University and concluded with eleven years of professional football with the Minnesota Vikings. These years included a Bakersfield City and a San Joaquin Valley Championship in high school, two national top-ten college rankings at Stanford, while winning Rose Bowl teams my junior and senior years. Finally, while we never actually won a Super Bowl with the Vikings, I had the privilege of playing on four NFC Championship teams with the Vikings, and playing in three Super Bowls and four Pro Bowls.

In spite of all of that wonderful and unexpected success, I will have to say that my "best" and most satisfying day on the gridiron was a fall, October day at Stanford Stadium before almost 90,000 people when we finally beat the USC Trojans (24-14) after having lost to them the previous 12 years in a row! The win finally got the "monkey off our back" and led to those two successive Rose Bowl victories and two national, top-ten finishes. While I was always much more motivated by team success over individual accolades, that "best day" against USC also earned me the National, Sports Illustrated Defensive Player of the Week which only made that victory and experience doubly satisfying!

—JEFF SIEMON
Minnesota Vikings, Four-Time Pro Bowl Linebacker

My two best days in sports: As akid growing up in Toledo, Ohio I was very unhappy. I felt I didn't experience the love many others did. Wanting to be a great football player, having Jim Brown as a hero, I thought if that could ever happen to me it will be the greatest thing in the world. That was my dream. As a kid even through high school I had to have my mother's signature forged. Only playing two years Pop Warner football I played no more until my junior year in High School. I thought my chances were not very good and because of the classes I took in high school, I did not think I was able to apply for college because of the program that I was in, it was for kids they thought would not graduate from high school.

But then I got a break, I was able to take the S.A.T. and was able to gain a scholarship to the University of Nebraska. My first greatest moment was as a sophomore starter, I was the defensive MVP for Nebraska's first ever national championship in the 1970 Orange bowl. I was on top of the world. My second greatest day in sports was when we beat the Cincinnati Bengels and won the 1982 SuperBowl XVII in Pontiac, Michigan before my home crowd once again, and I was on top of the world. My greatest day in life over 34 years ago when I gave my life to the Lord and Godprove to me that he was Real and that he was really God and gave me proof that he was God. He filled me with the power of his Holy Spirit and that was the best day I've ever experienced in my entire life. For which I am very Grateful !!!

—WILLIE HARPER
San Francisco 49ers, All-American Linebacker

I have two best days:

1) 1970 Game at Dallas Cowboys -we won 38-0. That's the good news...the bad news (for us) was the Cowboys won all the rest of their regular season games & went to the Super Bowl.

2) Game 10: 1976 vs Rams at the Coliseum. We were down 14-6 at half time and 28-27 with 4:32 left in the game... marching down into position for a Jim Bakken 25 yard Field Goal with 0:04 seconds left. I completed 13-16 passes in the 2nd half.

—JIM HART
St Louis Cardinals, Four-Time
Pro Bowl Quarterback

Every day is my best day. I am blessed to have my wife, our wonderful children & grandkids. I love what I do and am very fortunate to work in a tremendously inspirational environment, with outstanding coworkers.

Without trying to sound corny, God is in my heart and soul- always was and always will be. I am happy every day I can give glory to Him. It's the least I can do, for what He's given me and our family. Never stop trying!

—NICK STOCK
Green Bay Packers, Assistant Coach

1) Being inducted into the College Hall of Fame-1982
2) Winning the 1951 Sugar Bowl vs. Oklahoma
3) Being part of the New York Jets winning the 1969 Super Bowl III

—VITO "Babe" PARILLI
*New York Jets, Three-Time AFL
All Star Quarterback*

Best days:

1) My spiritual relationship & marriage to wife Marty
2) The memory that when I was 5 years old on Thanksgiving I was sent to my room to pray for forgiveness and that was the first time I relied on God
3) Athletically, when we beat Alabama in the Liberty Bowl and I had 225 yards and when I shot a 66 to win the Palm Springs Invitational.

—BOBBY ANDERSON
Pittsburg Steelers,1st Round Draft Choice 1970, Running Back

My greatest thrill was playing in the team of the Century in 1971-1972 football season. The preseason had Nebraska ranked number one, Oklahoma number two. That we remain that way throughout the season. Oklahoma was the last game on our schedule to that time it had been the greatest build-up of any college football game ever. They played on Thanksgiving Day in 1971. It was the only college on TV that day so we had isolated coverage. The game seesawed back-and-forth; all of the fans were into from the start to the finish,we got the ball with three minutes remaining down 31 to 28 drove approximately 70 yards and Jeff Kinney scored the winning touchdown with time running out to give Nebraska victory 35 to 31. The highlight for me was the third intense situation during that when one of our drives was when I hit Johnny Rogers with a 12 yard gain to keep the drive alive. Johnny Rogers also had a 70 yard punt return early in the game they gave us our first touchdown. To this day 95% of the questions that people asked me are a reference that 1971 game of the century between Nebraska and Oklahoma. I often wonder how my life would have been different had we lost that game. I guess we'll never know until you get to heaven and ask my Lord.

—**JERRY TAGGE**
Green Bay Packers, 1st Round
Draft Choice 1972 Quarterback

January 23, 2005 was the birth of my daughter, Charli and November 1986 vs. Arizona State, I ran for 104 yards on one interception. (voted by University of Arizona as the greatest Wildcat play)

—CHUCK CECIL

*Green Bay Packers, Arizona
Cardinals, Defensive Back,
Coached Tennessee Titans*

In regards to my best day, besides my wedding day and the birth dates of my three children it was when I had the opportunity to play in the Rose Bowl on January 1, 1971. I had the great fortune to play with Jim Plunkett at Stanford University and my senior year we won the Pac-10 a championship for the first time since 1952. In the Rose Bowl we were up against the number one team in the country that year, Ohio State, who was unbeaten and untied about 40 point favorites to win the game. I think all of the Stanford students and alumni were just happy that we were in the game and I doubt that very minute the thought we really have a chance. We ended up beating Ohio State and I was fortunate to catch the game clinching touchdown late in the fourth quarter. We won 27 to 17.

I grew up in Southern California and the thought of ever playing in the Rose Bowl was almost un-thinkable. It was the biggest football game of the year back then as it was no Super Bowl. I will never forget coming out of the locker room after the game and having my parents, girlfriend – now my wife of 37 years – and friends there to share the victory. It was an incredible day.

—RANDY VATAHA
New England Patriots, AFC
Rookie Team 1971,
Wide Receiver

My best day was when Coach Frank Leahy offered me a scholarship to play football for Notre Dame. That started a lot of wonderful things for me and I'll always be grateful.

—JOHNNY LUJACK
*Chicago Bears, 1st Round Draft
Choice 1946 Quarterback*

It has been difficult to write about a best day, as I have been very fortunate to have many best days. The day I was married, the day my first son was born, the first Steelers Super Bowl victory and all the Steelers this, my first game at North Catholic where I scored my first touchdown.

But I would say my very best day was in 1989 when the Steelers beat Denver for the AFC championship and several hours later my first grandson was born on Christmas;that day was the best day.

—DAN ROONEY
Pittsburg Steelers, Hall of Fame Owner

One of my best days, I recall, was against the Baltimore Colts in November 1960, when I played for the Detroit Lions. I didn't start, but entered the game in the fourth quarter; the score was 8 to 3; in favor of the Colts. I threw a 40 yard touchdown pass to Hop Cassidy; who caught the pass and ran into the Goal Post for six points.

Next series, we kicked a field goal to make the score Detroit 13 - 3 Colts game with two minutes 53 seconds on the clock. Johnny Unitas took Baltimore down the field and threw a 34 yard touchdown pass to Lenny Moore to take the lead 15 to 13. The Colts kicked off to the Lions with 14 seconds on the clock, and we returned to our own 35 yard line. I then threw a pass to our tight end, Jim Gibbons, with 10 seconds remaining; he went 65 yards, scoring the winning touchdown, Detroit Lions 20 Baltimore Colts 15. It was the last play of the game

—**EARL MORRALL**
Detroit Lions, Baltimore Colts, Miami Dolphins, Hall of Fame Quarterback

One of the best days I ever had was when we played the 49ers in Detroit. I had nearly 500 yards rushing.

—DOAK WALKER

Detroit Lions, Hall of Fame
Running Back

Every Sunday!

—GEORGE BLANDA
*Chicago Bears, Baltimore Colts,
Oakland Raiders, Houston
Oilers Hall of Fame Quarter-
back & Place Kicker*

In day where I'm smiling, the sun is out, God's in his heaven, my children have hope for a brighter tomorrow, and life transcends the mundane, that is my best day.

—TODD CHRISTIANSEN
Oakland Raiders, Five-Time Pro Bowler, Two-Time Super Bowl Champion Tight End

My best day: 1.Super Bowl XVI   2. Stanford 33 Notre Dame 16

—BILL WALSH
San Francisco 49ers, Hall of Fame Head Coach

As a young aerial gunner on a B-24 Liberator during World War II, after coming back from Germany on my 30th and final mission. I kissed the ground and it was all over: I survived.

—CHUCK BEDNARIK

Philadelphia Eagles, Eight-Time Pro Bowler, Hall of Fame Line Backer/ Center

Best day? Sports: Super Bowl XII January 15, 1978, it was my birthday and I was co-MVP with Harvey Martin. Not a bad day!

—RANDY WHITE
Dallas Cowboys, Nine-Time
Pro Bowler, Hall of Fame
Defensive Tackle

Best day partial list (take your pick)

Getting married

Two kids

Touchdown in Rose Bowl as an 18-year-old freshman

Getting out of the Air Force

Graduating from USC, 1949

Mom at her debutante ball

Making it in the Rose Bowl ago San Francisco 49ers

Spending the day with Pres. Ford

First Super Bowl

—**PAUL SALATA**
San Francisco 49ers, CFL
All-Stars, 1952 End,
"Mr. irrelevant"

120

When my daughter was born. Then I realized, and felt, unconditional love. She's given me purpose in life and the desire to be the best I can be in all endeavors.

—MARCELLUS WILEY
San Diego Chargers, Dallas Cowboys, Jacksonville Jaguars Pro Bowl Defensive End, ESPN Announcer

Too many days to pick out of best one, but:

Winning the 1938 NFL championship, winning 1956 NFL championship, beating Washington to get to the Super Bowl and winning it, beating San Francisco to get to Super Bowl XXV and upsetting Buffalo in it.

— WELLINGTON MARA
New York Giants, Hall of Fame
President and Owner

The best days of my life are: when I'm relaxing and fishing in the Sierra, above Yosemite, and can reflect on the good times with my family and friends.

—MIKE WHITE
Oakland Raiders Head Coach,
San Francisco 49ers, KC
Chiefs, St. Louis Rams
Assistant Coach

I hope my best day is yet to come, and I believe it is. My birth was my best day because without that having happened, nothing else will. I believe the best is yet to come in my life and saying that, I'm not being facetious, I have had the greatest life in the world. I have a great mother and father,great family, everything is great, but I think that there are some things that you just don't count on. It's not about football, it's not about business, it's not about wealth, it's about what you do for people and I think over a period of time the more you do for people the better you feel.

—MIKE DITKA

Chicago Bears, Dallas Cowboys, Tight End, Hall of Fame Head Coach

My best day was the Bears versus Redskins game in 1970; I scored an extra point to win the game.

—DICK BUTKUS
Chicago Bears, Eight-Time
Pro Bowler, Hall of Fame
Linebacker

I had a brother that was blind, and he used to say every day was a good day! My best day is: yesterday, today, tomorrow.

—DAVE WILCOX
San Francisco 49ers, Hall of Fame Linebacker

I have been extremely fortunate and blessed during my lifetime that I could give you about 100 best days. But if I could only pick one, I'd say it was January 2, 1997 when the Gators beat FSU 52 to 22 to win the first National Championship in Florida, and my first time as a head coach. It is what makes a championship so special is that you have so many people to share with: your family, your coaches, players, and everyone I call a friend.

—STEVE SPURRIER

Quarterback, San Francisco 49ers, Washington Redskins, South Carolina & University of Florida, Coach

The best day of my life when this bad breath of the doctors slapped me on ass with his cold hands and I screamed what the _____ are you doing? It was my first breath at that time and have been reading and enjoying life ever since.

—FRED WILLIAMSON

Pittsburg Steelers &Kansas City Chiefs, Three-Time AFL All Star Defensive Back

Professionally 1950 championship game, personally the day I met Bev.

—OTTO GRAHAM
*Cleveland Browns, Hall of
Fame Quarterback*

Thanksgiving Day versus the Cardinals.

—CLIFF HARRIS
Dallas Cowboys, Safety

It is difficult to define the "Best Day" in my life, as I have been fortunate with many such days. My best day professionally was Super Bowl XXX-IV followed by the day I was named head coach of the Rams and then the day I won my first regular-season game.

—MIKE MARTZ
St. Louis Rams, Head Coach,
Chicago Bears, San Francisco
49ers Assistant Coach

Happiest day was the victory Super Bowl VI, I had a pretty good game also. Best game Pittsburgh or Chicago in 1970 or 1971?

—BOB LILLY
Dallas Cowboys, Eleven-Time
Pro Bowler, Hall of Fame
Defensive Tackle

My most memorable day, to me, was against the game that all three of my children were at the Coliseum with my wife. She would take all 3 of them to one home game each year. That day I caught three passes for three touchdowns. It was a big thrill for me to have all my family in the stands that day.

—JACK SNOW
Los Angeles Rams,Pro Bowl
Wide Receiver

The best day of my football career was when I was enshrined into the NFL Pro football Hall of Fame in 1978.

—RAY NITSCHKE
*Green Bay Packers, Hall of
Fame Middle Linebacker*

Every day is my best day.

—FRANK GIFFORD
*New York Giants, Eight-Time
Pro Bowler, Hall of Fame De-
fensive Back, Flanker*

My best day was when the San Francisco 49ers beat the New York Giants 39-38 in the NFC 2002 first round playoff.

— JIM MORA, JR
Head Football Coach, Atlanta Falcons, UCLA

It is impossible for me to look over so many special times that I have had in my profession. I have been fortunate to work with some great teams during my career and look forward to many more "Best Days".

—JIM MORA, SR
Indianapolis Colts, Head Football Coach

My best day was the day I was named the head coach of the Baltimore Ravens. Another memorable day was the Monday night football game versus the Green Bay Packers. I was coaching for the Viking and our win broke the Packers 39 game home field winning streak!

—**BRIAN BILLICK**

Dallas Cowboy, San Francisco 49er Tight End, Baltimore Ravens, Minnesota Vikings, Coach

To me every day is my best day. Of course there been days that are especially best with my family and friends, each and every day provide me with all the love and understanding and encouragement I need to be successful. Of course there are also those days in the NFL when your team played and outstanding game and won. This is another best day.

—WADE PHILLIPS
Buffalo Bills, Dallas Cowboys,
Head Coach

Winning Super Bowl IV

—HANK STRAM
New Orleans, Kansas City
Chiefs, HeadCoach, Broadcaster

My best days were the Orange Bowl in 1963 where I was credited with 31 tackles and a 17 to 0 win over Oklahoma. Second, Super Bowl VI with a win over the Dolphins.

—LEE ROY JORDAN
Dallas Cowboys, Five-Time Pro Bowl Linebacker

I have been fortunate enough to have had many great moments. Two that stand out... The first being the 1955 USC versus Notre Dame game. We were heavy underdogs, and fortunate to score 20 points a record, and we beat them handily. A tie with that would be the 300+ yard gain I have against the Chicago Bears and when I was with the LA Rams. We broke and 11 game losing streak against them.

— JON ARNETT
Los Angeles Rams, Chicago Bears, Five-Time Pro Bowl Running Back

My best day was December 18, 1977 Dallas played Chicago in Dallas for division playoff game. That particular day our team line and I had maybe my best game as a pro. I intercepted three passes in route 37-7 victory. That represents an NFC record still stands and helped to contribute to the other reference I will, most interceptions in a playoff game.

—CHARLIE WATERS
Dallas Cowboys, Three-Time
Pro Bowl Defensive Back

Covering the Super owl in Miami (one of my favorite cities—lived there for quite some time) for Fox Sports. I was assigned to the Broncos. All of my on-air hits went perfectly and when the game ended I was on the field amongst the confetti, under a perfect blue moon. I felt very lucky!

—SUZY KOLBER
ESPN sportscaster

My best day is every day, because the gift of life that God gives us.

—BRIAN KELLY
Tampa Bay Buccaneers, Detroit Lions, Defensive Back

I passed 509 yards in one game versus the Chicago Bears in 1982.

—VINCE FERRAGAMO
Los Angeles Rams, NFC
Champion 1979 Quarterback

My best day as a Green Bay Packer was playing in the championship game for Green Bay after spending five years losing with the Los Angeles Rams. This was at the end of 1965 season I was able to catch a touchdown pass from Bart on a snowy day. Just being a member of a championship team was a best day.

—CARROLL DALE
Green Bay Packers, LA
Rams, Three-Time Pro Bowl
Wide Receiver

The 1950 championship game versus LA Rams I kicked a 16 yard field goal in the closing seconds for the game-winning point-final score: 30 the 28.

—LOU "The Toe" GROZA
Cleveland Browns, Nine-Time
Pro Bowl Place Kicker

Being inducted into the professional football Hall of Fame in Canton, Ohio.

—ELROY "Crazy Legs" HIRSH

Los Angeles Rams, Three-Time Pro Bowler, Hall of Fame, Half Back, End

I'd have to say my best day is the day I announced I was staying in school for one more year.

—RICKY WILLIAMS
New Orleans Saints, Miami Dolphins, Pro Bowl MVP 2002, Running Back

When my wife, who is a huge Magic Johnson fan, and I met Magic Johnson at a hospital benefit in Los Angeles. Turns out, Magic, was a big fan of my career with the Raiders and my light beer commercials. My wife was very impressed. It was a good night.

—BEN DAVIDSON
Oakland Raiders, Three-Time
AFL All Star Defensive End

My best day was the VJ day... August 1945, day World War II ended and I, along with 16 million others, came home to our families.

—MARV LEVY
LA Rams, Washington Redskins, Buffalo Bills, Coach, VP and General Manager

June 27, 1964 was my best day. I married my high school sweetheart, 35 years three children or grandchildren later, I realize what a special day it was. I also realized it was my luckiest day!

—DAN REEVES
Dallas Cowboys Running Back, Atlanta Falcons, Denver Broncos, Coach

My best day was when I submitted my life to the Lord at a young age. Our relationship has grown to great heights, all because I think yes to Jesus, who is my best friend. I spent just about all my days with Him, I'm doing His work, what a friend I have in Jesus.

—LEM BARNEY
Detroit Lions, Seven-Time Pro Bowler, Hall of Fame Defensive Back

I am going to take the liberty to split your request into two answers: my best day is yet to come, because I look forward to the challenge of upcoming projects, always with the knowledge that there are solutions for everything. I look on tomorrow as the best day opportunity. Regarding my best experiences particularly related to sports: my best day from the past was January 12, 1970 day after the Chiefs won the Super Bowl. It specifically relates to the victory parade and celebration the downtown area and onto the liberty Memorial in Kansas City. Thousands of fans congregated to be part of the event. The Chiefs winning in the game the day before was fun, but seeing the reaction of the fans was the icing on the cake for my best day.

—LAMAR HUNT
Hall of Fame Owner of the
Kansas City Chiefs,
co founder of the AFL

My College days were the best days of my life, and my Seattle days were the worst days of my life.

—BRIAN BOSWORTH
Seattle Seahawks Linebacker

My most exciting day as a pro football player was in 1974 when I was a wide receiver for the Portland Storm of the World Football League. I caught a touchdown pass in the late fourth quarter to tie the Chicago Fire in a home game. My best day as a pro was a few weeks earlier when I caught five passes for about 100 yards and a touchdown. On the touchdown catch, I ran a corner, my favorite pattern, from the right side of the formation. After breaking towards the corner looking over my right shoulder I had to adjust to the ball and ended up catching it over my left shoulder. This was the last time that I had a chance to visit Sam's Corner!

—SAM DICKERSON
Portland Storm Wide Receiver

For me, when you look at great stories about being an athlete, and being a professional football player, being the number one pick in the draft, all those things come to mind for a lot of people. They will say I guarantee that was the best day of his life. But it really, truly isn't. But for me, the best day was graduating from the University of Southern California, with my degree. My mom told me my junior year when I had an opportunity to forgo my senior year and go to the pros, was to stay in school and get my degree. I said, well, I've got a chance to make a whole lot of money, why would I do that? Because she felt, and I feel now, that graduating from school, whether I went on the NFL as the number one pick, that having that degree was going to make success for me and my family, the rest of our lives regardless. I might not have been an NFL Player, but I was going to have a degree, could walk into an office and say, hey I can get a job. I can do those things. It may not have been the millions and millions of dollars I could have made, but at least I had that piece of paper and nobody could take that piece of paper away from me for the rest of my life.

—**KEYSHAWN JOHNSON**
NY Jets, Dallas Cowboys, Tampa Bay Buccaneers Three-Time Pro Bowl Wide Receiver

I don't have one, I have two. I am just a kid from Cleveland Ohio, you grow up and your life kind of unfolds in front of you how it unfolds, and April 16th, 1995 I get Taylor Jackson, and January 8th, 2000 I get Morgan Jackson. I get those two right there, and I am blessed to have those two days in my life. They cause me some anxiety sometimes, but they are my best days.

—TOM JACKSON
Denver Broncos Three-Time
Pro Bowl Linebacker,
ESPN Announcer

...at Brown, in the audience, when the first of our two children, Meredith, graduated. Doug would be the very next year, but by then Kathy's mom had died. The three living grandparents were all there, the parents, watching, number 1 get a degree and number 2 is about to. Everyone that was important was still with us there, and it was three generations. When the kids graduate from college, you hope you have done a good job.

—CHRIS BERMAN
ESPN Sportscaster

I think about my son's, the day my sons TJ, Rex, Dante-the day that they were born, I knew I almost had a little mini defensive line in front of me, my guys...those are probably the best days of my life there.

—TEDY BRUSCHI
New England Patriots,
Pro Bowl Linebacker,
ESPN Announcer

Mine was making the decision to go on "The Biggest Loser" to be honest with you. It saved my life. Being a husband and father to seven kids, going through with that decision, has given me the opportunity to see my kids grow up and do all the things I always wanted to do. I think that I am grateful for that.

—DAMIAN WOODY

New England Patriots, New York Jets, Detroit Lions, Pro Bowl Offensive Lineman

I played for the original Dallas Texans 1960, Lamar Hunt was the owner & the coach was Hank Stram. I was the backup quarterback to Cotton Davidson. Playing an exhibition game I dislocated my right shoulder and it knocked me out for the year. The next year I was called into the Army ROTC and the Texans brought in Lenny Dawson. I did not return. I guess my best moment was that I got married to my beautiful wife, and have now been together 54 years. I went on to become a pretty good college coach. I won the S.E.C title in 1976 which is a miracle for Kentucky.

—FRAN CURCI
Dallas Texans Quarterback,
University of Miami-Tampa,
Kentucky Head Coach

I scored four touchdowns in the second quarter during my first game at Notre Dame against Indiana in 1951.

—NEIL WORDEN

*Philadelphia Eagles, First
Round Draft Choice
1954, Fullback*

Everyday!

—JOHN BRODIE
San Francisco 49er, Two-Time Pro Bowler, 1970 MVP Quarterback

I was drafted into the NFL as a Linebacker in 1971, there were only four linebackers taken that year. Isiah Robertson went in the 1st round, while myself, Jack Ham, Phil Villapiano were drafted in the 2nd round. When I got to the Detroit Lions, Joe Schmidt was the coach. I didn't start, there were guys like Jimmy Davis and Wayne Walker playing in front of me; and I was frustrated.

My 2nd year we were playing the Jets with Joe Namath as quarterback. It was the 4th quarter and we were ahead by one or two points; with less than two minutes to go in the game when Coach put me in. On the next play I intercepted a pass from Joe Namath. That was my best day.

I used to see that play on Funny Friday Finals, and I still jump up and down... I get goose bumps and I feel like I want to go play!

— CHARLIE WEAVER
*Detroit Lions, Washington
Redskins, 2nd Round Draft
Choice Defensive Linebacker*

December 3, 1987- The day my 1st was born.

—TERRY ROBISKIE
*Miami Dolphins,Oakland
Raiders, Running Back, Atlanta
Falcons Assistant Coach*

Dad played football at Michigan State for two years under Coach "Biggie Munn" and Duffy Daugherty and then went into the Army. The coaches wanted him to come back and play after service. Dad got poison ivy, and did not get shipped off to Korea. At the end of dad's service, he was a guest at the head table at some military service as Private, he ran into Biggy Munn. His old coach again tried to get dad to come back to Michigan State. Dad said he needed a job and was married; he could not take care of his family and play football. Biggie Munn promised to take care of dad if he would come play, so he did. But after the war, Duffy was head coach and Biggy was now an assistant. Biggy gave dad odd jobs to do too, which did not please Duffy. Dad did not finish at school, but still made the NFL through the backdoor. He was able to play for the Eagles & Bills, getting into the NFL even though he thought that dream was over once he went to war. Being able to realize a dream, even though it was not the direct path as envisioned, was a culmination of best days for dad.

—TOM SAIDOCK
Philadelphia Eagles, Defensive Linebacker As told by his son

I have been fortunate to have been on a National Championship team, Super Bowl Championship Team, and those moments were great, but they all pale in comparison to the days my children were born...four days, my best days.

—MARK BRUNELL
New York Jets, New Orleans Saints, Three-Time Pro Bowl Quarterback

My best days are when I played for the LA Rams, marrying Elizabeth and any time I can help someone else, My Deacon Jones Foundation and the AFC/NFC Championship fundraiser event allowed me to give back and brings me joy.

—DAVID "DEACON" JONES

LA Rams "Fearsome Four-some", Eight-Time Pro Bowler, Hall of Fame Defensive End

My best day was meeting my Lord & Savior Jesus Christ July 15, 1977.

—NEIL LOMAX
St Louis Cardinals, Two-Time
Pro Bowl Quarterback

When I received Jesus Christ- July 1995

—FRANK SANDERS
Arizona Cardinals, Baltimore
Ravens, 2nd Round Draft
Choice 1995 Wide Receiver

My best day were the days my two daughters were born

—WALT PATULSKI

*Buffalo Bills, St Louis Cardi-
nals, 1st Round Draft Choice
1972, Defensive End*

Making the Varsity High School Team as a freshman and scoring a touchdown the first time touching the ball. (65 yard run).

—JERRY LE VIAS
*Houston Oilers, San Diego
Chargers, AFL All Star
Wide Receiver*

Good to hear from you. My best day was when I was coaching for the Oakland Raiders in 1976. We had made the playoffs in 1972-1975 but never got to the Super Bowl. In 1976 we got to the playoffs again and beat the Steelers and Patriots to go to Super Bowl XI vs. the Minnesota Vikings. We beat them in the Super Bowl 32-14 and I'll always remember that day. Thanks for asking!

—BOB ZEMAN
San Diego Charges, Denver Broncos AFL All Star 1962 Defensive Back

Doing something you only could only dream of or see happen to others and having my wife, 2 daughters, my Mom, Dad, and cousin there.

—MICHAEL SPURLOCK

Tampa Bay Buccaneers, San Francisco 49ers, Arizona Cardinals, Wide Receiver

Being voted most valuable player of the 1953 World Championship Game –Lions vs Browns.

—DICK STANFEL
*Detroit Lions MVP World
Champion Guard*

The 21st Annual All-Star football game - college All-Stars vs the Detroit Lions at Soldier Field, August 13, 1954. I played the entire game; offensive quarterback and defensive half back. In 1954 the college players had to play both ways; to make the game even the Lions played college rules. The Lions still won going away, and I played the best game of my career.

—TOM "DUB" DUBLINSKI

*Denver Broncos, Detroit
Lions, Quarterback*

My best day was April 30, 2001. At 4:19 pm my son, Sidney Ellis Shoop was born after my wife Maria worked through 62 hours & 19 minutes of labor! I missed an entire three days of rookie camp to be with Maria every minute of her labor & on Sunday April 30th, the greatest prize arrived.

—JOHN SHOOP
Carolina Panthers, Oakland Raiders, Coach

Any day we can spend with our grandchildren.

—JIM BAKKEN
St. Louis Cardinals, Four-Time
Pro Bowl Kicker

The greatest day in my life was the day my daughter was born. I was in the room during delivery. Immediately after the birth someone said, I know you wanted a boy so that he can play football but you have a beautiful daughter. I had no preference of a boy or a girl, I just wanted a healthy kid. Immediately after birth I started counting fingers and toes and kept getting 11 of each in my excitement. After I calmed down I counted 10 each. I didn't get a boy so as to play football, but I got a girl that turned out to be a helluva soccer player that gave me just as much or more joy and pride

—CARVER SHANNON
Winnipeg Blue Bombers &
Hamilton Tiger Cats, Grey
Cup Champions; CFL, Los
Angeles Rams, Half Back/
Defensive Back

181

When I read your question I immediately thought to myself, how could watching my three children being born not be my "best day"? I have been blessed winning a Super Bowl in 1985 with the Chicago Bears and a National Championship in 1990 coaching at my alma mater the University of Colorado. But I'd take the birth of my children over those days any time. I've played in great college games and arenas as well in the NFL. I've played alongside greats as Walter Payton and Mike Singletary. But my greatest accomplishment can't compare to the birth of my children and the wonder blessings they are!

—BRIAN CABRAL
Atlanta Falcons, Green Bay Packers, Chicago Bears, Linebacker, University of Colorado Linebacker Coach

Being inducted into the Football Hall of Fame was the best weekend of my life. Being with all these guys all weekend. You cannot charm your way into the hall, can't finesse your way into the hall, it's the best.

—MICHAEL STRAHAN
New York Giants, Seven-Time Pro Bowler, Hall of Fame Defensive Lineman

You caused me to do some deep thinking with your question, "What was your best day?" I have several, maybe many, to select one is very difficult. My best days include my marriage, our adoption of two children, my employment with the Dolphins, my service in the Marine Corps, returning to college, my first college coaching job, my pro jobs with Baltimore, Miami, NY Giants, San Diego and Miami, and most of all my health.

I realize that has not helped you or have I answered your question. I am the first to admit, I have been fortunate to work with good coaches, good players and great fans. If I had to select one, it would be our win over the Washington Redskins to complete our undefeated season at 17-0 in 1972 at Super Bowl VII. It was something that has never been accomplished and to date it remains a record.

We had an outstanding group of players. They worked hard, they prepared, they practiced and they played the GAME.

Coming up with my best day has brought into focus what is really important, "lock out the past, and prepare to enjoy each day as the best."

—BILL ARNSPARGER
Miami Dolphins, Baltimore
Colts, Coach

184

I am not trying to be funny, my best day is always when I get out of bed in the morning.

—CHUCK ORTMAN

*Dallas Texans, Pittsburgh
Steelers Half Back, Punter*

I had many great days and loved them all.

—JIM OTTO

Los Angeles Raiders, Three-Time Pro Bowler,Hall of Fame Center

My best day was playing Washington in 1981 at RFK Stadium...I scored twice, recovered an 80 yard fumble and had two interceptions: one for 32 yards and the other for 72 yards; all with my mom watching in the stands.

—DWIGHT HICKS

Indianapolis Colts, San Francisco 49ers, Two-Time Pro Bowl Safety

In the Viking playoff games, I was the franchise's first 100- yard receiver. I led the team with 120 yards in winning our 1969 NFL Championship game against the Cleveland Browns.

—GENE WASHINGTON
*Minnesota Vikings, Denver
Broncos, Two-Time Pro Bowl
Wide Receiver*

God granted me talent on the field and it gives me great joy making others happy. All my days with happiness are best days.

—**CHRISTIAN "The Nigerian Nightmare" OKOYE**
Kansas City Chiefs, Two-Time Pro Bowl Fullback

Monday night (my day off)

—EVAN MOORE
*Seattle Seahawks, Cleveland
Browns, Tight End*

Every day is a best day, darling. I make the best of each day because health and success can turn in a blink.

— TERRELL OWENS

Dallas Cowboys, Philadelphia Eagles, SF 49ers, Six-Time Pro Bowl Wide Receiver

Winning Super Bowl XVI; going from the worst team in the NFL to the best. Making four tackles on the goal line stand at 1st and inches to the "STOP" at the goal line was big play.

My best day out of sports was the birth of both daughters, Ashley & Courtney, the best.

—DAN BUNZ
San Francisco 49ers, Detroit Lions, Two-Time Super Bowl winning Linebacker

Super Bowl XLIII

—PAT FLAHERTY
*New York Giants,Offensive
Line Coach*

Your request for a "best day" was easy for me BUT, I will give you two.

My personal best day was the day I married my wife Susan. I'm a very lucky man, and she makes every day the best day.

My professional best day was the 2004 NFL Draft, when we drafted Eli Manning and immediately traded him to the New York Giants.

—A.J. SMITH
*Executive Vice President/
General Manager, San
Diego Chargers*

Best Day Ever? February 1982-I gave my life to Jesus.

Best Moment? In football, my first Pro Bowl. Greatest Joy II? Being a husband and dad.

—TUNCH ILKIN
Pittsburg Steelers, Two-Time
Pro Bowl Lineman

To answer your question is easy for me. I assume you are asking about the best football game, and that would be Super Bowl V- 1971; Baltimore Colts 17-Dallas Cowboys 13.

—RICK VOLK

Baltimore Colts, Miami Dolphins Three-Time Pro Bowl Safety

My best day in football was, of course, Super Bowl
III and the championship years with Cleveland.

—WALT MICHAELS
*Green Bay Packers, Cleveland
Browns, New York Jets Five-
Time Pro Bowl Linebacker*

My greatest days in Pro Football are obviously ones. #1 winning the NFL Championship in 1951 with the L.A Rams and #2 with the NY Giants in 1956.

—ANDY ROBUSTELLI

Los Angeles Rams, New York Giants Seven-Time All Pro Defensive End, 1962 NFL MVP

I was asked to write about my happiest day in sports. Here it is: I played football in high school and then one year in Junior College because of my grades that needed to be made up to enter UCLA. I played for UCLA 1940·1943. I then had to go to war, so I joined the Navy. After the war I played one year for the L.A. Bulldogs. I was then noticed by the L.A. Rams, who just moved to LA.

My happiest football day was the day I joined the Rams. I played with them for five years, including a 1951 championship game. It gave me a chance to play with such players as Tom Fears, Elroy "Crazy Legs" Hirsh, Bob Waterfield, Norm Van Brocklin, Glenn Davis and so many more.

I am 90 years old and spent very happy moments remembering these exciting Ram games and the many friends I made through sports.

— JACK FINLAY
Los Angeles Rams, Guard

Believe it or not our victory over the Patriots in Super Bowl 42 was not my best day football, despite the magnitude of the game and the last minute drive to win it.

My best day was in 1982 when Southern Connecticut State University defeated Albany State University with a kickoff return for a TD with only seconds remaining.

I was the Head Coach of an undefeated team ranked #3 nationally in Division II playing the #1 ranked team in Division III; who were also undefeated. They had just scored the go-ahead TD with about 30 seconds left in the game.

They kicked off to us and tackled our returner for a small return. However, they were off sides and made to kick off again. With approximately 10 seconds left, we returned the kick for a touchdown. The complete change of emotion from total despair to complete euphoria made this my best day.

—**KEVIN GILBRIDE**
University of Connecticut,
New York Giants, Houston
Oilers, Coach

I would say my most memorable moment in my L.A. Rams career was during our World Championship game against the Cleveland Brown in the L.A. Coliseum. I was a defensive end specializing in the pass rushing. I tackled Otto Graham causing him to fumble. We recovered and went on to score. That play changed the momentum of the game. We ended up winning the game. It was great to be a World Champion.

—LARRY BRINK
Los Angeles Rams, Two-Time
Pro Bowl Defensive End

Best Day: When my first Daughter was born. She was unbelievably alert & strong. In the delivery room she raised her head up and smiled at me.

Best Sports Day: When we beat the Dallas Cowboys 26-3 to win the NFC Championship which allowed us to play in the Super Bowl 1972. I intercepted a pass and ran it in for a 42-yard touchdown.

—BRIG OWENS
Washington Redskins "Ring of Fame" Safety

I don't want to sound trite by I consider each day I wake up my best day. I have been truly blessed with so much more than I deserve a loving wife in Maggie; two wonderful children in Katie and Andy; a warm and comfortable home; three jobs that I never considered jobs: teacher, coach and administrator at Orange Coast College for 37 years, owner of six-nationwide summer Quarter-back and Receiver Camps; and a side judge in the NFL for 17 seasons. I've got terrific friends, a cov-enant group, two brothers, nieces, nephews, and a new son-in-law. I'll never forget the past week-end (12/2011) where Andy's USC water polo team won their 4th consecutive NCAA Championship with Andy scoring a goal against my alma mater, Princeton. In the semi-final and the SC crowd wildly cheering his goal.

I'll never forget my wedding day 25 years ago. Mar-rying Maggie was clearly the best decision I ever made. The day I got the call that I'd been hired at OCC for my first out of grad school was memo-rable. The birth of our children were other great days along with their first hair cuts, birthdays, go-ing to preschool, grammar school, middle school, high school and then off to college. The day that the director of the NFL football officials called me to say that I'd been appointed to the NFL staff of officials was another special day. The phone calls I received two years apart congratulating me that I'd earned the privilege of officiating Super Bowls XXXVI and XXXVIII were incredibly memorable. The day during the spring of my senior year in high school waiting to hear what colleges had accepted me and I received a FAT envelope from Princeton University was very special.

Staying up all night in June of 1964 on the United States Senate floor as a Senate Page while senators filibustered the landmark 1964 Civil Rights legislation was very memorable. I consider each day my best day (even though there have been a lot of not "best" days in the literal sense the death of my parents, brother, friends, pets…) because I have no idea what's in store that particular day. On March 16, 2011, I was playing golf with friends. I wasn't playing particularly well UNTIL the 16th par 3 when I got my first hole-in-one! I never thought I'd get one of those suckers and lo and behold! One never knows what's in store. Take one day at a time. Enjoy each and every minute we are alive. I try to remember to my wife and children every time I see them how much I love them.

—LAIRD HAYES
NFL Line Judge

The day I was inducted into the Pro Football Hall of Fame was the best day of my life. There I was, standing onstage, and when I looked out in front of me, I saw all my teammates, my parents, my wife and kids. It was a really special day for me to have the people that mean the most to me there. I was really emotional. To be recognized and singled out at that level, especially since I worked so hard to make it, plus getting to be in the company of the best of the best, is such an honor.

—DAN MARINO
Miami Dolphins, 9-time All Pro Quarterback, 1984 NFL MVP & Offensive Player of the Year, Hall of Fame

My best day was on May 10th, 2014, the day I got drafted into the NFL by the New York Giants. It's funny, because it was the most stressful day as well. I remember the day started out and I woke up early as I could barely sleep. I had my future on my mind and I had no idea what would happen next. The moment that my phone rang and I saw my name come across the TV Screen, I felt like a child again. My childhood dream finally came true.

I will be able to play the game I love for a living. Everyone I loved, family and friends, were around me that day and I got the opportunity to celebrate and enjoy the experience with them. I remember wishing I could hold that moment forever: the feeling of having a dream for as long as I can remember...and for it to finally come into fruition. That was the best day ever.

—**DAVON KENNARD**
New York Giants, NFC Defensive Player of the Week #14, 2014 LineBacker

I only played that one year with the Steelers, but my biggest thrill was playing in the All Pro Game in Los Angeles in 1955. But I enjoyed playing with the Steelers and for Mr. Art Rooney.

—JOHNNY LATTNER
Pittsburg Steelers ProBowl
Half Back

My best day? It would have to be the day the Baltimore Colts won Super Bowl V against the Cowboys. To have most of my immediate and extended family in Miami, plus a few of my closest friends, there to experience everything which transpired was truly memorable. Add to the fact that I played quite a bit and had a small part in the outcome of the game made it even more enjoyable. I never slept after the game‑ up all night partying. It is one experience in life that no one can ever take away from you. It is there from posterity.

—SAM HAVRILAK

Baltimore Colts, New Orleans Saints Defensive Back/Wide Receiver, Super Bowl V Champion

It was certainly winning Super Bowl III-Jets over the Colts. As a rookie free-agent-out of Harvard-playing in a game of that magnitude...it was certainly very special.

Right next to that moment would be the immaculate reception in Pittsburgh when Franco Harris scored the "Miracle Touchdown."

Add to that-an interception off Johnny Unitas when he was with San Diego. These would be some of the highlights...I still have the ball from that game.

—JOHN DOCKERY
New York Jets, Pittsburg Steelers, Cornerback

Congratulations on your giant project, you have a lot of courage.

My Best Day was the day we won the "World Championship" in 1958. Not because of anything I did, but because our team won the championship. We had a great group of players who were great people.

—JIM MUTSCHELLER
Baltimore Colts, Pro Bowl
Tight End

My best day is when I competed against the Giants. I intercepted a pass then ran a play back 65 yards.

My worst day was against the Cowboys, they were a real problem for me. In the last minute the end ran a down and up to fake me out. Clendon Thomas assisted for me and he did not score.

—BRADY KEYS
Pittsburgh Steelers, Minnesota Vikings, Pro Bowl Corner Back

I think it was 1964 when I had one great day against the Bears. I had a big day and was happy because George Halas (owner of the Bears) traded me to the Vikings.

—BILL BROWN

*Minnesota Vikings, Chicago
Bears Four-Time Pro Bowl
Running Back*

My best day would be the day we adopted our first son, Blake, then the birth of our second son, Mike. The bringing my granddaughter, (born 90 days premature) home from the hospital, who is now a happy, healthy 6 year old.

—STEVE OWENS
Detroit Lions, Pro Bowl
Running Back, Heisman
Trophy Winner

My best day in sports was December 17, 1967... my first year with the Chiefs and the last game of the year. In the first half Denver was kicking the ball six and seven yards into the end zone. Just before taking the field, Coach Hank pulled me aside and said the Denver players were pulling up because they did not think I would run the ball back. Well, Hank was right, after getting the ball six yards into the end zone I started up the middle of the field and with good blocking I cut to the left side line and went for 106 yards touchdown and a new AFL Record.

Also, my roommate was Mike Garrett ˙he set a new Team Record for rushing and Otis Taylor set a Team Record for receiving and that was my best day in sports.

—NOLAND "Super Gnat" SMITH
Kansas City Chiefs, Wide Receiver/Return Specialist

1) 1966-George Allen named me #1
2) 1967 Bears-Colts-last game of the season to finish 11-1-2, and the Colts finished 11-1/2 but because of their loss to us, we went to the play-offs! The Colts stayed home!
3) 1973-Philadelphia Eagles-I was named chairman of Eagles Fly for Leukemia. We raised $600,000 to help first McDonald House in US and helped build research wing for Leukemia at Children's Hospital.

—ROMAN GABRIEL
Los Angeles Rams,
Philadelphia Eagles Four-Time
Pro Bowl Quarterback

My best day, it is hard to say. To limit it to one would be unfair. But I do know it would involve seeing someone else being made happy by something I did.

—RON RIVERA
Chicago Bears, Linebacker,
Carolina Panthers Head Coach

My fondest memory of my football career was the day I started and played the whole game of Super Bowl X as a rookie. The game was played in Miami, my home state, with all my family and friends there.

—BURTON LAWLESS
Dallas Cowboys, Detroit Lions,1975NFL All Rookie Team Guard

You and I are a couple of lucky guys, you've got Laurie and I've got Sophie! We have been married 63 years. Your story is amazing. I hope our paths cross one of these days. My best day in football was always the days we won! Its 11 guys on offensive and 11 guys on defense. Football is not "me", but "we".

—FRED "Curly" MORRISON
Chicago Bears, Cleveland
Browns Pro Bowl Running Back

I actually have two Best Days.

1st:November 3, 1968: My punt of 84 yards against New Orleans. It is a record for the Cowboys that still stands today, but that's not the real reason. My wife was watching on T.V. and got excited, jumped up in the air and two days later my 1st son was born.

2nd: January 16, 1972: being a member of a World Championship Team. It's hard to describe what it means to have that ring and memories to last a lifetime.

—RON WIDBY
Dallas Cowboys, Green
Bay Packers Pro Bowl Punter

Best Day in football? Running back a kickoff for 99 yards for a touchdown for the Redskins and I held the record for some years.

—DALE ATKESON
(as told by his wife, Wanda)
Washington Redskins Fullback

Three times in my Football Life were "best days". My senior year in High School we won the game we had to win to attain our goal-the district Championship. It was close but we held on (a goal line stand) to win 13-7

The 2nd "best day" came in the 1959 world championship game when the Colts beat the Giants in overtime 23-17.

The 3rd "best day" was winning the AFC Championship in 1985 Patriots 31- Dolphins 14. We were defeated by the Bears in Super Bowl XX.

The most significant day in my life happened just before going to camp in 1960. I have been the recipient of God's gifts: My dad & mom, second, my wife Sally, 3rd my precious children: Mark, Suzanne, Ashley and the list goes on. Thank you, Lord.

—RAYMOND BERRY

Baltimore Colts Six-Time Pro
Bowl Wide Receiver, Dallas
Cowboys, Patriots, Detroit
Lions Coach, Hall of Fame

In 1972 I was a fifth round draft choice of the St. Louis Football Cardinals out of the University of Wyoming. I was cut the day before the first regular season game. During the second game of the season the starting right guard was hurt and the Cardinals resigned me to a contract.

During training camp I was the only rookie on the offensive line. Dan Dierdorf (Michigan) and Tom Banks (Auburn) were starters and they spent my entire training camp experience making life difficult for me. It was difficult for me to understand why it was so important for them to haze me in this fashion.

I couldn't understand why they would do this to a teammate. In fact I considered them to be two of the worse people I had ever met. I disliked them with an intensity that is greater than you could imagine.

When I returned 8 days later and became the starting right guard two weeks later, I still didn't trust them at all. These were two of the worst people I have ever met. But things changed during my first start for the St. Louis Football Cardinals. The coaching staff had me playing on all the special teams unit both defensive and offensive.

In fact I even blocked a punt during that game against the New York Giants played in old Yankee Stadium. I was running every offensive play and every special team.

At half time Tom Banks and Dan Dierdorf went to the offensive coach "Bill Austin" and asked him to remove me from all the special teams because it was wearing me down. This was the first time they had ever done anything that would help me and that is when I felt that I had arrived in the NFL. That these two assholes would stand up for me and tell the coach that what they were expecting of me during the game just was not fair.

To this day both Dan Dierdorf and Tom Banks are two of my closest friends and we talk at least twice a month, if not more. Oh, By the way, I continue to remind them what a bunch of pricks they were when I was starting my career.

That was the big lesson "don't let the turkeys get you down." I was accepted by this group and we continued to play side by side for the next 6 years and were classified as one of the best offensive lines to be assembled in the NFL. We tied an NFL record for only allowing 7 Quarterback sacks in an entire season. Other than my 6 years and all the games and the three different teams I would play on over 10 years is what I was say was "MY BEST DAY" It was not what I did but what others did for me.

—CONRAD DOBLER

Cardinals, New Orleans Saints, Buffalo Bills, Three-Time Pro Bowl Lineman

One of my best days ever was the 1977 AFC Championship game between us (The Denver Broncos) and the Oakland Raiders. It was a frozen field and our 1st time in the playoffs. The Raiders were a perennial powerhouse and were expected to win their trip to another Super Bowl, but as fate would have it, the game was played at Mile High Stadium in Denver! We also were a very good football team as well. It was a brutally tough and physical game but the Broncos prevailed and we were off to our 1st Super Bowl. The city went absolutely crazy, which was why it was so much fun, it wasn't a team going, it was a whole city. I was a corner that year, starting for only my 2nd year. It was magical. It was the start of a great run for the Denver Broncos.

—STEVE FOLEY
Denver Broncos, Corner

My Best Day was when I was elected captain of the Navy Football Team in 1945.

—HENRY R. DUDEN

US Navy, Single Wing Quarter-back & Linebacker

With all my experiences in football game, Super Bowls and such, my best day without a doubt was on December 15, 1962 when I married my soul mate, Carolyn. It has been 49 years and she has been by my side through it all.

—BILL CURRY
Green Bay Packers, Houston Oilers Center

I'm approaching my 68th year and have yet to have one best day. Don't pull out the Kleenex though—I've been fortunate to have a job I love together with a never-ending passion for my work to every day for me is my best ever! The worst days of those who enjoy what they do are better than the best days of those who don't.

—STEVE SABOL
President, NFL Films

I have had more than my share of surgeries from sports, but I feel like a "beginner" after reading what you have been through the last 17 years.

I would say that the "best day" I have ever had was the day I married my wife, Karen. She knew a cousin of mine and who was in the travel business. At that time, in 1996, I was single and had been married more than once. So I was not looking for any more close relationships.

So, I guess my Best Day was April 7, 1996, the day I met my wife. I had some wonderful days in sports, but none that were more meaningful than that day I met Karen. That may not be they type of answer you were expecting, but, after thinking of it for a short while, I came to that decision.

The sports year were wonderful, but not as meaningful as meeting my wife.

—TOMMY MASON
*Minnesota Vikings, Los Angeles
Rams, Washington Redskins, #1
Draft Choice1961, Three-Time
Pro Bowl Running Back*

My best day with the Chicago Bears was being traded to the Washington Redskins. With the Bears I had taken over for Brian Piccolo when he died (my worst day and season) and led Gale Sayers to the rushing title. I then got traded, which was very good for me as George Allen for the Redskins (Over the Hill Gang) was also a Christian and righteous guy who could develop me personally and professionally.

Best day with the Redskins was winning the NFC Championship, and playing in the Super Bowl.

—MICHAEL HULL
*Chicago Bears, Washington
Redskins Fullback*

Best day in Football? Very hard to break that down after playing high school, college, and pro football, thinking back to my rookie year with the L.A. Rams, one of the great thrills for me was the 1st time I was introduced in the starting lineup at the L.A. Coliseum before 70,000 fans.

—JOE CAROLLO
Los Angeles Rams Pro
Bowl Tackle

My best sports day ever was a 1978 win over Oklahoma, Being from Nebraska I grew up watching this rivalry. I was in high school when Nebraska beat Oklahoma in 1971 in what many call the game of the century. Anyway, Nebraska had not beaten Oklahoma since 1971 when I was then a senior and captain of the Nebraska defense. We pulled out a thrilling victory which still gives me goose bumps when I think about it. The game was recently voted the #1 game ever played in Nebraska's stadium history. I've included a short summary from a Lincoln paper.

"Best memory was being carried off the field by fans as Oranges were coming out of the stands. It represented a trip to the Orange Bowl. My first." Believe it or not, as circumstances sometimes lead, we had to play Oklahoma again in the Orange Bowl and lost.

— GEORGE ANDREWS
Los Angeles Rams Linebacker

As far as my best day in football, that's a hard one. My personal best was probably 1983 opening game against Buffalo. I got four sacks in their home stadium. Also made some tackles but can't remember how many. Another personal best was in your backyard against the 49ers also in 1983. I forced a couple fumbles late in the game and sacked Montana at least once to help with the win.

My fondest memory was beating the Jets in the Orange Bowl to go to Super Bowl XVII or maybe it was Super Bowl XIX, the games kind of run together.

—DOUG BETTERS
*Miami Dolphins Pro Bowl
Defensive Lineman
1983 Defensive Player
of the Year*

My best day in football was when I was named team captain for the 9th time in the 11 years while I was with the Houston Oilers.

—RAY CHILDRESS
*Houston Oilers, Dallas
Cowboys Five-Time All Pro
Defensive Lineman*

I don't have a best day experience other than winning the Super Bowl to finish a perfect 17-0 season. But after reading about your life, I am now a certified Mark Keys fan!

—**BOB KUECHENBERG**

Philadelphia Eagles,
Miami Dolphins Six-Time
All Pro Guard

I have co-best days. In 1976 and 1984 the Vikings won the NFC Championship game at Met Stadium in Minnesota in front of all of our fans and my family. It was two very great days for me and the team.

—STU VOIGT
Minnesota Vikings Tight End

My best day in the NFL with the 49ers was the Cleveland Browns game in 1949. I intercepted two of Otto Graham passes. We won 56-28

—PETE WISMANN
San Francisco
49ers, Linebacker

I think back on all the exciting moments that I was fortunate to experience in the NFL and the best day I remember was the first Monday Game the Denver Broncos played in. For two years we had been trying to get the eye of Howard Cossell and the NFL to give us a chance to play on Monday Night Football. We started the 1973 season off kinda of shaky but after a couple games we were on a winning streak and we were picked to play the Oakland Raiders on Monday Night Football.

The game was close for three quarters and with less than five minutes to go, the Raiders scored to go ahead 20-17. With about two minutes on the clock we got the ball on our own twenty yard line. We ran a few plays that got us close to the fifty yard line. With less than thirty seconds on the clock we were able to get within field goal range for our kicker Jim Turner. There was no time on the clock, he kicked about a thirty-five yard field goal to tie the game. Since there was no overtime at that point, it went into the record books as a tie. The Denver Broncos had their first Monday Night Game end in a tie. I will always remember my first Monday Night Game. That was one of My Best Days!

—**MARVIN MONTGOMERY**
Denver Broncos, New Orleans
Saints, Atlanta Falcons
Offensive Guard

My Best Day was playing in Super Bowl III in Miami, Florida.

—WILLIE RICHARDSON
Miami Dolphins, Baltimore
Colts, Two-Time Pro Bowl
Wide Receiver

I have not yet had my best day. But, if you were to say my best day in the NFL, lets look at my greatest day. To be great it means to me that one overcomes great obstacles. When you overcome great obstacles, then you become great, then that day becomes great. I would have to say that day was in 1982, when the San Francisco 49ers had gone to the Super Bowl against Cincinnati. At that time it was Super Bowl XVI in Detroit, MI. Cincinnati was favored and they were supposed to win. They had even already given the MVP Trophy to Cincinnati's quarterback. We had a guy named Joe Montana and so I'm building up to the forward of my "greatest day".

We were coming to the game and it was snowing and icy and all that type of stuff. A group of us left early and the other group left at the earlier time and they got stuck in traffic. We were there and my greatest day was that I asked God for a victory in the Super Bowl and because I believed he would give it to me he did give it to me. I went to the board in the locker room, and in those days they had chalkboards, and I wrote on there "we are champions." I wrote it and spoke it because you have to have a belief and you have to have faith. That particular day where God answered my prayers was a great, great day on great terms. There were over a 100 million people watching

240

that game. So I told Him if he gave us the victory, then I would give him the glory. As soon as we won the game, and everyone was congratulating us on a great game we had played. I looked and saw the Lombardi Trophy, so I went and got it. And because the camera goes where the Lombardi Trophy goes, I held it and once I held it, the camera operator came over and they were obligated to ask me a question. I think it was Brett Musburger and he came and started to ask me a question, I started with; "first of all I would like to thank God for this victory." It was my best day just sharing that victory. God had heard my cries, God had heard my prayers, and He had answered it. It didn't take a year, it didn't take six months, he answered that day. I was truly thankful for that. So, he has blessed me. I have had great days but that is my best day.

—**CHARLE YOUNG**
Philadelphia Eagles, LA Rams,
San Francisco 49ers, Two-Time
All Pro Tight End

I have had a lot of good memories over the years but the day I got drafted to the Dallas Cowboys was "My Best Day".

Family is a huge part of my life and it can be extremely difficult to get everyone together at one time. What made the draft day so special was that my entire family on both sides were there to support me, something that had not happened for quite some years. On top of that I had all of my closet friends present to join in on the festivities. It's a good thing both sides of the family like to cook because we had a house full of people with huge appetites. My family cooked up a storm and we all ate like royalty for the entire day.

Of course, the whole purpose of having everyone together was to hopefully celebrate some good news. I had done pretty well at the combine and had spoken with a few teams, but kickers aren't drafted as often as any other positions so it can be a hit or a miss. Thankfully for me I got a homerun. At about two o'clock in the afternoon I got a phone call from Mr. Jerry Jones himself. With all eyes on me I walked outside with fear I would not be able to hear Mr. Jones and Coach Phillips over the cheers and whispers. On April 29, 2007 the Dallas Cowboys officially offered me a position on their team. All of my hard work and practice had finally paid off and I was getting the chance to live out a dream of playing in the NFL. I know how fortunate I am to have this opportunity, but without my friends and families support I could not have had my "Best Day."

—NICK FOLK
Dallas Cowboys, New York Jets, Pro Bowl Kicker

I had many good memories in the NFL. I played well against my younger brother, Fred, once in Kansas City, he was with Chicago and once against the Houston Oilers vs San Diego in Balboa Stadium. We were both on special teams. He was returning punts and I was San Diego's safety, he was about to go for a touchdown and I stopped him—the announcer said that nice run back was by Glick, he laughed and said, "and he was stopped by Glick." I can't match up to your injuries, Mark, but I have had bad knees, back left shoulder, broken jaw, and lost teeth to remind me.

—GARY GLICK

Pittsburg Steelers,
Baltimore Colts, San Diego
Chargers Safety

What a worthy work you have done to share players "Best Days." Ray is in heaven with his Lord and Savior Jesus Christ. He died on April 19th, 2012. If he were to answer your question, he would unequivocally say that his best day was Sunday, October 23, 1977 when the Falcons played the Bears in Chicago. He had two picks and a touchdown pass deflection; limited Walter Payton to 69 yards rushing, nice individual tackles, one assist, 2 touchdown-saving tackles. Our friend, John Hilton, who was coaching the Bear's offense said that their half time in the locker room was spent trying to figure out how to stop Ray.

—RAY EASTERLING,
Atlanta Falcon Safety.
As told by his wife, Mary Ann
Easterling

Atlanta Falcons, Safety

My best days were:

*Marrying my wife May 5, 1990

*The birth of our daughter Rebecca on December 1, 1993

*Running onto the field as a member of the Buffalo Bills on January 27, 1991 for Super Bowl XXV

—GARY BALDINGER
Buffalo Bills, Kansas City Chiefs, Indianapolis Colts, Defensive Tackle

Opening game of the 1950 season:

We, the Cleveland Browns, had been champions of the All American Conference and The Eagles had been champions of the NFL. This was the setting of the big game, we won!

—**W.A. "Dub" JONES**
Miami Seahawks, Brooklyn Dodgers, Cleveland Browns, Two-Time Pro Bowl Halfback

November 1969, my senior year of college at North Texas State. There were two games remaining in the season. At the point in the season I had 22 sacks. I wasn't really on the NFL radar. We played Tulsa and I ended the game with 11 sacks and a defensive touchdown. I recorded five sacks the following week and ended the season with a total of 38 sacks. By the end of the season scouts had become aware of me. I was invited to play in the Blue/Gray game where I recorded four sacks and the Senior Bowl. That year, Joe Greene was drafted #1 in the first round by the Pittsburg Steelers and I was drafted #9 in the first round by the San Francisco 49ers.

—CEDRICK HARDMAN
San Francisco 49ers, Oakland Raiders, Oakland Invaders (USFL), Two-time Pro Bowl Defensive End

Thank you for the invitation to participate in one of your "Best Day" endeavors.

My best day was my wedding day 59 years ago to my dear wife. My most memorable day-best day in football was the 1955 Championship game against the Los Angeles Rams in L.A.

This game was the most memorable because:
- After playing a season in sunless, cold raw days on frozen fields in the east coast and midwest, it was pure joy to be able to play on a warm, sunny day on green grass
- The 100,000 attendees each paid $5.00 to produce the largest pay-off purse to date of $3,200 per player. This was comparable to one-third of an entire years salary.
- It was a real honor to be able to play in the last game of the Hall of Fame career of Otto Graham.
- We won

—DON COLO
Baltimore Colts, New York
Yanks, Cleveland Browns,
Three-time Pro Bowl
Defensive Tackle

I have been lucky in that I have had so many best days-from the first win at Northwestern University to the Super Bowl win with San Francisco; to being named Head Coach at Stanford and later with the Viking. They are all moments I will never forget.

—DENNIS GREEN

BC Lions Halfback, Head Coach Minnesota Vikings, Arizona Cardinals

1. Receiving my kidney transplantation July 4, 2004 at Stanford Hospital in Palo Alto, CA.
2. Being the first player on a professional football team, as a member of the Baltimore Colts in a game against the Washington Redskins. I blocked a 40 yard kick (field goal) attempt at the cross bar, before the ball went over.

—R.C. "Alley Oop" OWENS
San Francisco 49ers, Baltimore Colts, New York Giants Wide Receiver

My greatest moment was Notre Dame/USC game 1973. I'm a freshman playing against our number 1 rival. The Trojans. They were ranked slightly higher than we were, but we were both ranked in the top 10. They had all stars: Lynn Swann, Pat Haden, J.K. McKay, Sam Cunningham, Richard Wood... well they were loaded. Our campus was going crazy with signs, hanging models of their players from their dorms roof. It was the greatest, most hyped game of the year. All I knew is that this was a big stage for a Big Game. Out of pure fear on the first play of the game S.C. tried a bubble screen to Swann. I got to Swann just as the ball and ripped Swanns helmet off! After that it was on. I ended up with 2 interceptions, a fumble recovery, and a knocked down pass. By far my greatest moment!. Thanks to God I did what God put me on this earth to do.

—LUTHER BRADLEY
*Detroit Lions, NFL, Chicago
Blitz, Arizona Wranglers USFL,
Corner Back*

There were many great days and experiences in my career as an NFL player. As we know with great days there are days where we struggle but through the grace of God we never give up.

It is very difficult just to pick "one day". So for me it was our (my wife Kia) relationship with Carroll and Pat Dale. Carroll was a wide receiver the Packers for at least 9 years when we came as rookies in 1970.

He was part of the glory years with the Packers: The Vince Lombardi Era. Coach Lombardi passed away in September of my rookie year. We were the new kids on the block.

When we first met them they were very gracious and helpful to us. We had a lot to learn!

As our friendship grew we noticed that Carroll and Pat were a little different from others in a good way.

How they handled adversity, how they treated each other and how Carroll lead his family. Carroll invited me to go to NFL chapel. I did not even know that existed in NFL. They are services held on Sunday Morning in our hotel for anybody on the teams to come to. They were non-denominational. The speakers were either local businessmen or former NFL players. I decided to go one particular Sunday because we were playing the Bears at 1pm and I needed all the help I could get! So I went to church on Saturday night and Chapel on Sunday. I was playing the "church game" at the time.

It was through NFL chapel and the speakers that I learned that God loved me unconditionally. They all knew they fell short of God's standards. But God sent His so Jesus to die for them and become sin on the cross. He wanted a personal relationship with them. They knew they did not deserve God's Love that could not earn or buy it. It is unconditional. They invited Christ into their lives, repented and committed their lives to Him so he could work through them to accomplish His plan from them.

I did that and went back into my church and it became alive. My had too's became my want toos. This is how we have navigated the trials and tribulations of life as a couple, as a family and now as a widower.

—MIKE MCCOY
*Green Bay Packers, Oakland
Raiders Defensive Tackle*

In my case, my best day in football came on January 27, 1991, when I was fortunate enough to be assigned to Officiate the Super Bowl Game in Tampa, FL between the AFC Champions Buffalo Bills and the NFC Champion New York Giants. It was the Silver Anniversary Super Bowl game, Super Bowl XXV, with all the pomp and ceremony surrounding such a special event.

To compound the intensity of the situation, the United States was involved in the Gulf War at the time and so security was a huge concern all week leading up to the Sunday game. We all flew into Tampa with our families on Thursday prior to the game. My family included my wife, Dauna, and our two young adult children, Sheri and Steve. Also, waiting for us when we arrived was longtime friend and former PAC8/10 football official Fred Gallagher. Fred had always told me that when I got my first Super Bowl assignment he would be at the game. The problem was that even though we got him a ticket to the game, he hadn't found a place to stay. So we made arrangements for a rollaway bed to be brought into our room and Fred stayed with us. Here we all were for 4 nights-all 5 of us in a small Marriott hotel room. It was like YMCA Family Camp and I'm getting ready to work the biggest game of my life. But we had a great time and it worked out really well.

The Officials are busy with meetings and various obligations during the days prior to the game but the NFL has things for the families to do all the time. Everyone was also involved in the dinners and functions that were held each evening. ON game day, we all left hours ahead of kickoff to go to the stadium. Because of the security issues, everyone entering the stadium had to go through a magnetometer,

Either stationary or hand held. With 80,000 fans, it took fours to file into their seats. The officials checked in at a special gate so we were in the locker room 3 hours before kickoff. The pregame festivities started early so by game time the stands were full. Each fan was given a small American Flag to hold and wave. The Officials came on the field for the coin toss and we split off into two groups, each group moving to a sideline to prepare to escort the Captains to the center of the field for the toss. I was on the Buffalo sideline with their 3 Captains. Standing with us was former NFL Commissioner Peter Rozelle, who was going to toss the coin. Helicopter Gun Ships with sniper protection were circling above the stadium. The stage was set for the most stirring and emotional rendition of our National Anthem ever presented at a Super Bowl game. With 80,00 fans waving their flags, Whitney Houston delivering the Classic Anthem and there wasn't a dry eye in the stadium. Steve Tasker Special Teams Captian for the Buffalo Bills, turned to me and said, "This isn't just another game, is it." What a moment. The game itself went really well. No problems. Both teams played solid football. The score went back and forth all night. It came down to a final drive by Buffalo with a minute left in the game. The Giants were ahead and Buffalo drove to the New York 29 yard-line with 8 seconds to go and Scott Norwood missed a field goal wide right by 6 feet—final score NY Giants 20-Buffalo Bills 19. We all met at the hotel after the game and everyone involved went to the NFL post game dinner and party. The perfect ending to a "Best Day in Football in the NFL" That is, unless you are a Buffalo Bills fan.

—**SID SEMON**
NFL Official

I am pleased to describe my Best Day in the NFL. It would have to be when I was playing for the Washington Redskins in 1982, and we won Super Bowl XVII in the Rose Bowl.

1982 was a crazy year—the season was shortened because of the strike. I was the Redskin Player Rep and a member of the NFLPA's bargaining committee, so it was a hectic fall for me.

Once the strike ended we went right back to playing football. We played only 9 games in the regular season and held a "Super Bowl Tournament" for the playoffs with 16 teams making the playoffs. We were the 9th seed, and hosted 3 games at RFK Stadium. The whole season went by so fast, it was a blur, and there was no week off between the championship game and the Super Bowl.

I remember when I ran out onto the field for pregame warmups thinking that I had never seen a more beautiful setting for a stadium. It was also a great day from a weather standpoint. The game against the Dolphins was hard fought and we ended up pulling away at the end, highlighted by John Riggins touchdown run on fourth and one. For me, though, the highlight of the day was when I was able to celebrate the victory with my father, Hugh "Big Murph" in the locker room. I still have no idea how he made it through the NFL security to get down to our locker room, but it made for a special moment.

My second best day in the NFL was when the Green Bay Packers won Super Bowl XLV in Dallas and I celebrated the victory with my son, Brian. I was sure that my father, who died in 2008, was smiling down on us.

—MARK MURPHY
Washington Redskins Pro Bowl
Safety, Green Bay Packers
Administrator

This is a rough question, because it challenges me to scan all the moments that stick out as "best." For me, "bests" need to be categorized. And there are lots of them. And best day in football encompasses many dynamics for me to scan and evaluate.

My best day in football was during my rookie year. Summer camp was very tough physically and very tough emotionally. Double sessions back in the 69 through the 70s—early 80s, was grueling with constant live practices, hitting was an expected reality for the players. It was sort of like training camps for gladiators. Live contact was expected. Tackling was not permitted to running backs or receivers during drills, except during scrimmages. Scrimmages were live. Two a days were above 2 hours each during the heat. Chuck Noll loved practice and loved to hear the pads and helmets pop. He would go around seeing who had chips of paint off their helmet and who didn't. In other words, who could really hit. Head blocking and tackling was taught as a technique, down field blocking was unlimited even below the knee. Quarterbacks were free game.

From all this rookies whittled down, veterans disappeared in the night, one rookie had every man on a sheet of paper taped to the wall next to his bed. He would mark them off as they got cut or traded. Ironically, he was the last man cut that training camp. Then he came back the following year and played another 9 years including winning two Super Bowls before he retired.

We sweated about 8-10 pounds of fluid per practice. As a tight end, I ran a lot. Fortunately I was in very good condition before I arrived. I could bench 365lbs and ran a 4.7 on grass with helmet, short and cleats. I was small for a tight end. I was 6'2" and weight about 220. But, I could block and busted my butt on special teams. After 5 pre-season games we were down to 47 players, 14 of us were rookies. With one pre-season game to go, that week was one all of us suffered through. Who was next to receive the ax? The news came to me by default. We were never sure until we read it or were asked to go see the coach. But, on our final Friday practice before the team would leave for Detroit to play the Lions, Chuck Noll read off who would be the Captains for the game. First was the offensive captain, which was Larry Gagner, our All Pro guard. Then our defensive captain, Andy Russell, our All Pro Linebacker. And to my great and complete surprises, Noll read out, Bob Adams our special teams Captain. I had to restrain all of my reflexes to jump out of my chair. I said a prayer that the plane would land safely in Detroit so I could experience being a Captain of a pro-football team out there in the middle of the field—flipping the coin for the kickoff advantage. I could not wait to call my family to tell them I'd made the team. It was one of those "too shaky to put the coins into the phone" moments. That was my first Best Day. Though I had many best days, that final week in rookie training camp was a 10.0 on the hyper scale. For emotional exhilaration, that was the best. A factor making it so exciting for me—I did not play but 17 minutes of football in high school, I did not play college ball till my junior year in a community college and somehow I received a scholarship to the University of the Pacific and played for the Tigers for 2 seasons. I was captain of the team my senior year. That was my previous "Best Day." I was not drafted by the NFL or the Army. However, Art Rooney Jr, the son of then Chairman of the Steelers, scouted me at Pacific, and advised Chuck Noll to sign me as a free agent, which he did! And that was the beginning of my most memorable BEST DAY IN FOOTBALL.

—BOB ADAMS

Pittsburg Steelers, New England Patriots, Atlanta Falcons, Tight End

My best day is when Harland Svare, the Coach of the Chargers, told me that I made the team. I was a free agent and worked extremely hard. The knock on me was that I wasn't fast enough and I was too political. In other words, I read a lot, so I had my own opinions on things. Too be a pro-athlete, especially in those days, you could not have opinions on society, nor know anything about the history of America and the treatment of Blacks. It was said in my family that Markus Garvey was my dads brothers Father and my Great-Grandfather was President of his back to Africa movement in the 20's. So history was always argued in my family when I was growing up. I was just supposed to be an athlete. I knew that was why I wasn't drafted.

When I first went to the Chargers I had to talk with the defensive backfield coach, Willie Wood. Willie told me to sit down and said to me that he heard I didn't like white people. I told him I don't know how that could be true since my roommate at the time was white and I was from Minneapolis Minnesota and their certainly were not many blacks in Minnesota. I told Willie that it seems to me that if you like yourself; some white people think that you don't like them.

—REGGIE BERRY
San Diego Chargers Defensive Back

The birth of my three children and my seven grandchildren. Maybe even more so the marriage to my wonderful wife of nearly 55 years.

—JOHN DAVID CROW
St. Louis Cardinals, San Francisco 49ers, Pro Bowl Half Back

M_Y Best Day(s):

November 13, 1994

September 24, 1996

August 22, 2000

The day my three sons were born!

—SCOTT LINEHAN
Miami Dolphins, Minnesota
Vikings Offensive Coordinator,
Los Angeles Rams Head Coach

I have two what I consider 'best days." The first one is as a player and the second as a Head Coach both with the Oakland Raiders.

In 1963 the Raiders began the season coming off a 1-13 1962 record. Al Davis was the new coach and I was coming off a year of convalescence (lung disease). Going into the last game of the season we had a 11-3 record. It was the second best record in the AFL with only San Diego better. In those days there were no wild card games so only the Champions of the Eastern and Western divisions would meet for the Championship.

If we were to win and San Diego to lose we would be the Western Champs as we had beaten them twice that year. Our final game was in our home stadium, Frank Youell Field. The opponent, the Houston Oilers with George Blanda as the quarterback. It was one of those wild and crazy games with whomever had the ball last usually wins. At half time the score was 35-35. We were happy and Blanda was furious.

With very little time left we had the ball and the score was 49-49. Blanda had thrown for 5 touchdowns and I had thrown for six. With seconds remaining, our kicker, Mike Mercer, kicked a field goal and we won the game. Mercer was the hero as

was the entire team. We did not make the Championship game, San Diego won their contest. They
played in the final game and demolished Boston
to become AFL Champs. Boston had finish tied for
first in the East with a 7-6-1 record. They won a
playoff game to take the Eastern Division.

We were obviously disappointed but in reality, the
Raiders became a force and I had my best day.

The next day was as Coach of the 1980 Oakland
Raiders. After starting out 2-3 we were facing a
tough remaining schedule and our starting quarterback, Dan Pastorini, had just broken his leg.
In steps Jim Plunkett, and as history shows takes
us down to the wire. We ended in New York playing the Giants. We were 10-5 and needed to win
to make the playoffs as a wild card. Once again,
we were battling the Chargers for the Western
Division of the AFC. We won and because of the
format became a wild card.

We beat the Houston Oilers at home in an upset.
Stabler and Casper were with them at that time.
(we had traded them earlier that year) Our next
game was in cold, cold, cold Cleveland (39 below).
Once again we were the underdogs but managed
to win in a very tight game 14-12.

That put us in the Championship at San Diego. With Fouts, Winslow and company they were clearly favorites to win and go to the Super Bowl. Well, with retreads like Plunkett, Bobby Chandler, Raymond Chester and company we beat them 34-27. On to the Super Bowl in New Orleans and we faced the Philadelphia Eagles and the great Dick Vermeil.

Once again we were big underdogs. However, this group of wild and crazy guys with supposedly no discipline managed to make no mistakes and win Super Bowl XV by a score of 27-10. Plunkett was the MVP and because of all the obstacles that were over came in only my second year as a Head Coach, I had my best day as a coach.

— TOM FLORES
Oakland Raiders, Buffalo Bills,
Quarterback, Oakland Raiders,
Head Coach

Rome, Italy July 9, 2005

I awoke at 6:30am, kissed by Fiance and went for a jog through the city of Rome. After breakfast at the hotel with Maria, I dressed in my Navy Blue Suit and tie, and she put on her beautiful white laced "wedding dress". The bride and groom took a cab and headed for St Peters Square, The Vatican-St Peter Basilica. We were to be wed at 10:30am by Monsignor James Checcio, who was the former team priest for the Philadelphia Eagles. We were directed to the Chapel of the Choir, and it was beautiful. There was Maria, myself, our priest, a photographer, organist and 2 witnesses. Seven wonderful people for the most Perfect Wedding. Maria and I exchanged vows, took pictures, music playing-it was Perfect! We went to have lunch and drinks at outside the city in the countryside. After lunch we explored Rome, and Monsignor Jim knew a hidden spot that made the day even that much more special. The day flew by, and we ended the evening with a meal in downtown Rome. Dining with my new beautiful bride Maria Spagnuolo!

This experience was completely divine intervention as 24 hours before our flight to Rome the paperwork for our wedding did not come through. It's a complicated story, but by the grace of God we were able to schedule a 10:30am wedding in the Vatican Chapel. Unbelievable! Monsignor Jim had petitioned the appropriate decision makers and our miracle happened.

My best day ever!

—STEVE SPAGNUOLO
New York Giants, Baltimore Ravens, St Louis Rams, Defensive Coordinator

Your question "what was your best day?" is very simple for me to answer: "every day I wake up is a chance for me to become a better person, a better father, a better husband, and a better friend." Football gave me an opportunity of a lifetime, it also gave me a platform to speak out and help other people better their lives.

Is it a great day when you help your team win and you had a couple of QB sacks? Of course it is, but it's a better day when you talk to a person about the courage to overcome their illness and they take your words to fight another day.

Is it a great day when you are a part of a National Championship team at the University of Alabama? Of course it is, but it is a better day when you witness the birth of your first child.

Is is a great day when you're inducted into the College Football Hall of Fame? Of course it is, but it's a better day when someone tells you, "thank you, you saved my life"

So, life is a gift we can all share, we can take our best day and make it even better by not thinking of ourselves. My best day is when I make a difference in the eyes of others.

—MARTY LYONS
*New York Jets, First Round Draft
Choice 1979, Defensive Tackle*

My best days were being with teammates:
Atlanta Falcons: John Small, Claude Humphry &
Bob Berry

Minnesota Vikings: Ron Yary, Ed White, Mick
Tinglehoff, Allan Page, Fran Tarkenton, Jim Marshall San Francisco 49ers: Cedrick Hardman, Jim
Plunkett, Paul Howard, Craig Mortha, Lyle Alza-
do Teammates, going into battle that is truly inspirational. I did not have a car wreck, but, games
against the Rams, Fearsome Foursome, Purple
People Easters, Dooms Day, Steel Curtain all left
me with plenty of injuries to heal from, now I "old"

— ANDY MAURER
Atlanta Falcons, New Orleans
Saints, Minnesota Vikings, SF
49ers Tackle

I have a lot of memories of sports best days. They range from the games at different friends houses as a youth to the organized teams of the catholic schools/leagues, high school & 5 years playing in college to my games in the pros. Overwhelming streak.

In 1969 the Falcons drafted me as a outside line-backer. I had played defense at Kentucky in the 5-4 format with the defensive ends dropping back, nothing in pass coverage at times. I came to camp and I was not very good in the pass coverage, so they moved me to offensive center. They had 120 people in camp looking for a job. There were 6 centers and I was the #6 center. Every day in practice I would hustle in every drill, gave all out effort and beat all the offensive lineman in spring at the end of practice. Little by little, they cut the squad down, I only played scrimmage teams in the first four exhibition games. In the 5th game, Norm van Brocklin gave me the start against the Boston Patriots, I think at Boston University Field. If I remember right, I think Nick Buoniconti was starting at MLB before he was traded to Miami and backed up by JimCheyunski. They played a lot of over and under defense and I had a good day. I was in great shape, as I learned how to train and lift weights in college. I had natural quickness and weighed about 235. As veterans, maybe their defense wasn't playing as hard as they could. For three quarters I played the greatest game I ever played at center in my whole career. Pass protection was flawless, I cut block and scrambled the DT over me all day, I slipped out on the linebackers. It was as if I was in the zone, blocking everyone I faced.

I never played a game as good as that 3/4th of the game. All the preparation and practice of the position, seven years came together that day. In Boston, the next week I started at home against the Redskins and Sam Huff at home in Atlanta. I spent the night trying to tag Sam, he spent the night O-Laying me and making tackles. I stunk that night.

—JEFF VAN NOTE
Atlanta Falcons, Five-Time Pro Bowl Center

I am thankful for the opportunity that Dan Rooney and the Pittsburg Steelers organization gave to a team 54 years ago to honor them. Our 1947 Steelers team was the first playoff team in the franchise.

I have had so many best days that it would be unfair to just pick one.

—GENE HUBKA
Pittsburg Steelers Running
Back/Safety/Punter

There were a number of "Good Days" making it difficult to pinpoint one in particular. Near with me for my reasoning in choosing a best day some 30 years after my last year in 1958.

I started playing in the NFL in 1954 for the Baltimore Colts for four years and ended with a final 5th season with the Chicago Cardinals. During this time the salary contract for me started at $5800.00 and ended at $8500.00 per season which was about the 12 team average of $7000.00 or so. There was not a player's union so you followed the rules set by the 12 owners and Commissioner, Bert Bell, such as buy your own shoes, pay your way to training camp, and getting reimbursed using rail fare (100.00 from S Dakota to Baltimore) If you made the team, it was deducted from your 1st game check.

A pension was started in 1959 excluding all pre-1959ers with a minimum of 5 credited seasons into the pension plan. (that excluded appx 750 players) Using the formula of 60.00 x 5= $300.00 per month. Thus March 1, 1987 was my best day with a small check as a reminder that we had not been forgotten and some satisfaction of being reimbursed for shoes and travel as well as a check

every month for life which has since increased
several times to $1870.00 per month.

—DOUG EGGERS
*Baltimore Colts, Chicago Cardi-
nals Linebacker*

I have been very fortunate during my lifetime. I have a wonderful family, a wife for 53 years and all blessed with good health. This has been possible due to many "best days".

The same holds true in my life in the NFL. A lot of people have been responsible for those "best days." Just for me personally, I would probably have to say that all of my best days were capsuled the day I was inducted into the professional football Hall of Fame. I thank all those who made that "Best Day" possible.

—TEXAS SCHRAMM

Los Angeles Rams, Dallas Cowboys, Hall of Fame Executive

I wish you well in your new endeavor, and I would have to say my best day is every day. Life offers so much it would be impossible to pinpoint a particular moment, and keeping a positive outlook provides for numerous opportunities. Character and integrity are the goalposts of life. It is difficult to fail when you have those attributes on your team.

—RALPH WILSON
*Buffalo Bills, Hall of
Fame Owner*

In my business career, my best day was beating the Steelers in Pittsburg to advance to the Super Bowl.

In my personal life, I would have to say I've had two best days...the days on which my two sons were born.

—DEAN SPANOS
Executive President & CEO San Diego Chargers

On May 29th, 1956 I lost my father to a plane crash in Monterey Bay, Ca. His Fury three jet was losing power and he had to make a last decision on to whether to eject from his plane, or to ride it in. He was a test pilot for the Navy. It was Memorial Day weekend and the beaches were filled with people. His last words on the microphone were, "This is November Pappa 88." (His call sign) "Taking it in." That day marked an important milestone in the life of his unborn son. Me! A month later I was born without a father in my story. Years later my mother told me that the night before my father died he was reading his bible and took out a red pen and circled a single word in a story.

My best day started with a devastating moment with my mom and an ache that I carried in my heart of never getting to meet my birth father. Like so many men I meet, I struggled with my identity, my sense of purpose and in my abilities as a father. Boys are designed by God to blessed by their fathers, and when they are either unable, unwilling, or are suddenly taken away, it leaves an ache in men instead of their fathers smile. It didn't matter how many things I achieved in my life. I couldn't win enough football games to fill the hole left behind my absent father.

The single word that my father circled in the bible

was in the story in the book of Matthew that he told about a storm, and sinking boat and a man who seemed to be walking on the water towards them. I was standing in front of a group of young people when I read them this story forty years after my dad died. In the story Peter saw what he thought was a ghost until he heard Jesus's voice. Peter said, "If it is really you! Command me to walk on the water with you" Jesus said, "Come". That was the single word my father circled that night laying next to my mom. When I read that story out loud to the kids I was in front of, that word jumped off the page and I heard the voice of the Father in heaven say, "The last word you father heard before he died was 'Come'. You are my beloved son, who I love."

Those words overwhelmed my heart as I stood in front of my high school group. I'm now somebody's son and all I needed to be complete as a man was poured into me by the only perfect Father that there is. I was rocked by the Fathers love, and have given the rest of my days to seeing that everyone I meet without a dad, they can have the best Father ever! That was my best day ever!

—ED MCGLASSON
New York Jets, Los Angeles
Rams, New York Giants,
Offensive Lineman, Center

I had two great days with the Denver Broncos:

1) 1972- Floyd Little Day
2) 1975- My last game at Mile High Stadium; we played the Eagles; after the game Bill Bergey and Harold Carmichael walked over to wish me luck. And to say that I was one of the best football players they had ever played against.

I never forgot that.

—FLOYD LITTLE
Denver Broncos Running Back,
3-Time Pro Bowl, Hall of Fame

The day I was drafted

—STERLING SHARPE
Green Bay Packers, Wide Receiver, 5-time Pro Bowler

My best day was as a quarterback at the University of Colorado when I completed the Hail Mary pass to defeat Michigan 27-26 in 1994.

—KORDELL STEWART

Quarterback, Pittsburg Steelers, Chicago Bears, Baltimore Ravens, Pro Bowler

My best day was when I playing for the Washington Redskins and we beat the Dallas Cowboys in our home opener in 1963. I had three interceptions, the first a 78-yard scoring run off a Don Meredith interception. Quarterback Norman Snead, and our offensive stars Don Bosseler, Dick James, Bill Anderson & Pat Richter played great. My second interception was late in the 2nd quarter; a diving catch that I could only scramble for an additional seven yards. The final interception was when Dallas was driving and with 1:46 left in the game; our wingback, Lonnie Sanders, deflected the pass intended for Frank Clarke, and I ran it back 25 yards to hold them off. We won 21-17.

I admitted after the game that I was hurt in the Ram game the week before; I had a bone chip on my right leg. John Sample had knee trouble, and with Claude Crabb's knee injury, Dick James was forced to play on defense. Things were bad enough without letting them know I was hurt. Playing hurt ended up being my best game, and my best day.

— JIM STEFFEN
Detroit Lions, Washington
Redskins Defensive Back

I wish I had a best day. I feel so blessed to have had so many great days in life. If I had one it would probably have to do with my family. My little nephew or niece—perhaps with my parents. I can come in to contact with all sorts of interesting people. Like you & your wife. I know this wasn't very specific, but it's the best answer I could come up with.

—RICH EISEN
ESPN NFL Total
Access Sportscaster

My best day was in 2003 when I was told that I was cancer free. In 1970 we had to win the last five games to get in the playoffs. Monday Night Football in Los Angeles was the last leg. I was beat for a touchdown early in the game. I had a great game other than that play, including an interception. We won the game and the next week we beat Green Bay 20-0. Those five weeks and that Monday was as good as it gets.

— **MIKE LUCCI**
*Detroit Lions, Cleveland
Browns Linebacker*

I was fortunate to play at USC and play for both the 1962 National Championship under John McKay and was captain of the 1963 USC National Championship team. Coming out of college, I was drafted by two California teams, the Los Angeles Rams in 1964 NFL draft as well as the same year by the San Diego Charges in the AFL draft. It was a thrill to be drafted by two teams, and two Southern California teams since I grew up in Long Beach was a kick. I chose the Rams, and only played pro ball for a few years. It was also a thrill to have my brother, Ollie, be the first person to be drafted by the expansion team, San Diego Padres.

—WILLIE BROWN
*Los Angeles Rams, Philadelphia
Eagles Wide Receiver/Half Back*

I was traded to the Cincinnati Bengals from the Denver Broncos in 1969 just before summer camp to find a struggling football team. The Quarterbacks were not the kind to make you a winner and Paul Brown was doing his best to make the offense fit the talent of the Quarterbacks.

Greg Cook had been drafted by Cincinnati and arrived at camp after the College All Star game and it was like somebody sprinkled magic dust on the field. Bill Walsh was the Offensive Coordinator and was developing a new offense that became known as the West Coast offense. The offense immediately began to gel and the team's confidence immediately began to grow solely because of the talent of the new rookie Quarterback Cook. Walsh worked with Greg like an artist painting a canvas....l can still hear Walsh counting the progression of the receivers, "one – two – three". From then on my best day was Sunday whenever Greg Cook was at quarterback. l knew we could win against anybody, and no matter what was called in the huddle l had a shot at Greg throwing me the ball. We would break patterns and Paul Brown would not come down on us as players. Greg Cook made me feel like l could walk on water.

—ERIC CRABTREE
Denver Broncos, Cincinnati Bengals, New England Patriots Wide Receiver

My biggest game as a New Orleans Saint was actually two games. My job for 13 years was to block first then be a receiver second. I was a good blocker and took great pride in being able to block the best NFL defensive end's and outside linebackers. I also had great running backs to block for: George Rodgers, Earl Campbell, Reuben Mayes, Dalton Hilliard, & Craig "iron head" Hayward which like the O-line you take great pride in when they would get 100 yards rushing in a game and over 1,000 yards for the season. But, being a tight end you are not measured by your blocking it is the catch's people remember.

Hence, my 2 games:
The first we were playing the St Louis Cardinals in the Super Dome in September 1984, which was my 4th season. If I was lucky I would get one or two balls thrown my way. Well, on this day I had 6 balls thrown my way caught all 6 --one being my longest reception of my career, 54 yards but I got stopped on the 4 yard line. It was question mark type route the linebacker got fooled, the rest of the defensive back field had jump our outside receivers, so I took an 20 yard catch and got 34 yards. It what we use to called YAC, yards after the catch, which was also a record for me. I caught a few more then we had 3rd down from about the 18 yard line they were in cover two and I was able to beat the safety on a cor-

ner route I made a diving catch in the corner of the end zone. My sixth and final catch was converting an 3rd down on the last drive to run out the clock it was a 10 or 12 yard out that help seal the victory. I finished the day with 6 catches, 1 touchdown and 131 yards which were personal bests at the time the 131 yards was the most yardage for my career Kenny "the snake" Stabler was our Quarterback in that game.

The second game that stands out, again because of receiving, but more because it was against our most hated rival—the Atlanta Falcons in the old Fulton County Stadium. It was the end of September, it was very hot but the Braves were done with their home games so we did not have to deal with the dirt infield which was great. Today's players do not have to deal with dual sport stadiums like we had to, you were just happy when they were 100% grass. My first catch was on a 4th and 1, we were on about the 35 yard line. They called a play-action pass play, I ran a deep corner. Everyone bit on the fake and I was able to convert the play for a first quarter TD. My second catch was from the 25 yard line, again they were in cover two and I was able to beat the safety to the corner of the end zone for my second TD of the game. I don't recall my third catch but my 4th was again a 3rd down to keep our driving going at the end of the 4th quarter which helped us seal an 17-14 win! I finished with four catches 2 TD's and 111 yarders receiving; Richard Todd was our Quarterback that day.

—HOBY BRENNER
New Orleans Saints Tight End,
1987 Bro Bowl

My best day was when I made it to the NFL and I could tell my mother she no longer has to work. Ever since I was a kid I told my mother if I ever made it or was successful in anything, I was going to take care of her. I made it to the NFL and was able to buy my mom and dad a house and take care of her financially like she did for me. My dad and six other siblings.

—JAMES STEWART
Jacksonville Jaguars, Detroit Lions, Running Back

Oakland Raiders win over Vikings-it was our team's first Super Bowl win in the team's history. Beating the Steelers in the AFC Championship that season was a close second. The Steelers of the 70's won 4 Super Bowls. The "Steel Curtain" may have been the best ever defense. Our offensive line was Art Shell, Gene Upshaw, Dave Dalby, George Buelter & John Vella-we were voted best ever offensive line.

—JOHN VELLA
Oakland Raiders, Minnesota
Vikings Offensive Tackle

Growing up my Family didn't have a lot. We had the necessities, as I'm sure a lot of Families did.

Out of the blue I told my Mom and Dad. If I ever made any money I would buy them a house.

My Best Day was in the summer of 1973. I was able to make a dream of a young kid come true. That was the year I was drafted by the New England Patriots. We as a Family were Blessed. It puts a smile on my face whenever I think about it!

Fight On

—**SAM CUNNINGHAM**
New England Patriots Full Back, 1978 Pro Bowl

My best day was throwing a record-setting 7 touchdowns against the Baltimore Colts September 28th, 1969. It is still a record today, I am tied with Payton Manning, Nick Foles, Sid Luckman, Y.A. Tittle, George Blanda, & Adrian Burk.

Another best day was that I was Head Football Coach for my alma mater, University of California-Berkeley during the famous game called "the play" Cal vs Stanford; Cal had five-laterals on the kickoff return to score the winning touchdown while dodging the Stanford band on the field.

—JOE KAPP
Quarterback, Minnesota Vikings,
Boston Patriots, Pro Bowl 1969

My life to this point has been a continuation of my best day as a Trojan. I can remember like it was yesterday, the whole recruiting process. The trip to Notre Dame with Marty Patton, meeting Sam Cunningham at the CIF Track and Field Championships, talking with impressive Dick Vermiel at Stanford and the imposing Tommy Prothro at UCLA. All these events were crammed into the process of choosing which University I would go to, free of charge, to play a sport I had come to love, get an education and meet the woman I would marry. On campus, it was like daily portraying a part in a feature length movie. Like the ones I had watched about the Gipper or Red Grange or Jim Thorpe. The cast of characters in this epic was unique and well defined. There was Rod Humenik, Willie Brown, Craig Fertig, Dave Levy, and of course; John McKay. And these were just the coaches. The players were equally fascinating and talented. But it was the atmosphere of USC... that was it!!! The mere fact of being there in the hallowed halls where all the prior greats had walked, studied, bled, lost and won. It was the whole thing. The dorms, the old locker room and training facility and the wood trimmed coaches offices. It was all part of the setting of this magical experience we were having being Trojans.

One of the seemingly minor items that had an impact on me was the bell. It tolled regularly, calling out the hour, quarter hour and half hour, I believe. It also served as a constant reminder to me that we were in reality and not in some dream state. The same bell was heard by everyone on campus and even some in the neighborhood. It communicated in its own way the importance of what our mission was at USC. Play the highest quality and level of football the way it was meant to be played and get an education. The education part was something that was a family necessity. My parents stressed it and it was almost automatic that we; all nine of us children of Robert and Julia McNeill, would get a college education. These items were at the forefront of my mind.

But the best day of many best days as a Trojan was this particular day In my second year at USC. We were staying in one of the dorms at USC as we were in the throws of fall training camp. During our off time some of the new incoming girls had come over to our dorm to meet some of the players. There was one girl in particular who caught my eye. Her name was Pamela. It would take some time before we would get to the point of becoming husband and wife and it was all my fault. It wasn't until the 32nd year of our marriage the full impact of the incredibly excellent occurrence meeting my wife.

The event that caused that awakening was me getting tonsil cancer. I elected to have surgery to remedy the cancer issue. The day I checked into the hospital at USC Medical Center at 5:00am I ran into a former teammate who was also having a minor procedure. I always look for confirmations in life that to me act as markers or signposts that let me know I am on the right track. Some would call them coincidences but I saw them as much more meaningful.

My surgery that day lasted for 10 hours and the first thing I remember when I awoke was seeing my wife smiling at me. She has the most wonderful smile. When I saw that smile I knew I was going to be ok. But it was what happened during the 12 days I stayed in the hospital recovering that helped me to fully understand how special was the day I met Pamela. I had undergone some very delicate and serious surgery by the excellent USC team. My recovery involved some pretty substantial pain meds that resulted in me having some very strange and frightening dreams. I would wake every night around 3:00am terrified and my wife would be right there. She stayed by my side for 12 days, sleeping in a small chair next to my bed. I don't think I would have made it through that ordeal if she had not been there. I really owe her my life. That makes the day I met her indeed My Best Day as a Trojan!

—ROD MCNEILL
USC Tail Back, New Orleans Saints, Tampa Bay Buccaneers

Acknowledgement:

I would like to thank the following people for their support: My wife, Laurie, my daughters Page and Megan, my mom & Don Shiel, Frank Bruder & Glenell Parker

And as always, the inspiration provided by the memory of David "Bucko" Shaw.

Dominique Goodrich and everyone at ESPN, Trent and the crew at TKO Generators, Sam Farmer; Sports Writer LA Times, Joe Bockrath, Steve Virgen; Sports Editor Daily Pilot, Sam Dickerson, Charlie Weaver, Charle Young, Marcus Allen, Cass Winthrop, Sam Havrilak at 4th& Goal, Lem Barney, Tommy Mason, Jim Taylor, Laird Hayes, and all the players and coaches who have supported me, Rick John, Kevin Lindsay, Mike Wilsey, Heather Hendrickson, Chris Clark, George Kerr, Joe & Roberta McCarthy, Joseph & Marjorie McCarthy, Cristina Roe, Jeff Farmer & Family, Shirley & Greg, Dr. Safman & Naomi Porter, Dr. Yaru, Dr. Carlson, Dr. Rhie, Dr. Bae, Dr. Ng, Dr. O'Carroll, Dr. Bruss, Dr. Stringer, Dr. Wynn and all the staff at each doctor's office, Paul Salata & Family, The Ed McGlasson Family, The George Andrews Family, The Byron Nelson Family, Rick & Trish Shepherd, Jesse Meinke & Family, Halla Mansour, Ron Lamerton & family, Blain Skinner, Sean Boulton, Diane & Jerry Tagami, and the Entire Helfrich Family.

About the Author:

Mark Keys is a Southern California native, residing in Costa Mesa with his wife Laurie, daughters, Page and Megan, their dog, Fumble, and two cats, Lucy and Ethel. Mark loves that his mom still lives at the beach in Newport in the house he grew up in, and he spends a lot of time there with her & the girls; and loves walking the beach. He played basketball growing up, in High School, and beyond; as well as body surfed until he injured his back. Mark is an avid reader, enjoys watching classic movies & westerns, collecting film and sports memorabilia, walking and listening to Rat Pack music. He also loves to travel and going to sporting events, when health permits. In spite of his numerous surgeries, including 6 back, 9 ankle, 9 knee, and 2 shoulder surgeries, he also experienced shingles, pneumonia, MRSA Staph infection, he has no immune system and fights continuous headaches and other health issues every day. But, through all of this, he keeps a positive attitude and outlook to make each day, his best day.

Made in the USA
San Bernardino, CA
11 January 2016